# SUCCESS BLUEPRINT

*FAST-TRACK YOUR SUCCESS BY MASTERING THE SECRETS TO SUCCESS AND CHANGE YOUR LIFE*

## Vanessa Gowora

*For Tatenda Gumise and Vaughan Taesean Morte*
*who believed in me before I believed in myself.*

# Table of Contents

# <u>Why I Wrote This Book</u>

Every kid has a dream: something out of this world that no

one understands. What happens is that dream fades away, or
is simply forgotten before they turn eighteen. At seventeen, I
wanted to be a writer. That should have been enough, having
a dream is like being in a candy shop, but the problem with
dreams is doubt. It's so easy to believe a lie because of
insecurities and I believed I wasn't good enough. My friends
said otherwise, but I saw them as being biased. So instead I
went to a university In Malaysia to study
Hospitality and Tourism.

Every class, I dragged my feet and I couldn't wait for the
day to end. When people asked me what I was studying the idea
of telling them was terrifying. I just wanted it to be over
- for the years to speed past, but they didn't. I then went to
do Events Management which seemed to be less painful, but
deep within I knew this wasn't for me. For my internship, I
went to South Africa and it hit me that this wasn't

something I wanted to do. I disliked being there, but I dragged through the days and months.

I had lost the fire I had as a kid and I had no idea how to get it back. Every day that passed was a sign I was getting closer to the end of the month. The internship ended and I went home to do another internship. It was a different company and I didn't enjoy being there. I spent the past two years applying for jobs in London, Los Angeles, and Vancouver.

Whenever I got an interview, it just disappeared and I spent those two years thinking it might be best to build an events company in my country. The idea was numbing and pondering about it made me uncomfortable. I didn't get anything, but a sickening feeling that I was going back to being a zombie.

I realized that I didn't want to do events, what I wanted was to live a life where I could make an impact. I wanted to be part of something more, it didn't matter how long until I got there I would get there. The problem was not with the profession, but with my lack of passion. I was done pretending to be someone I wasn't. For too long I had lied to myself that I could do this, but reality hit that If continued down this path I would regret it.

I noticed that many people (especially in their twenties) were doing jobs that they didn't enjoy, all because society tells us to and they were not living to their full potential. I was sick and tired of seeing many people with dreams, not doing anything with them because of fear and doubt.

A number of questions entered my mind: what gives me the right to tell anyone what they should do when I'm not living up to my potential? Who would listen to me? What do I have to offer?

Truth is, I was a very insecure person, I disliked myself and thought I was the worst human being on earth. My ADHD (also called a learning disability,) didn't help and I constantly struggled in school, I didn't have a name for it until much later on. There were a lot of dark moments when I thought the best thing was to give up on life and myself. I won't bore you with the details on how bleak those years were.

Primary school should be a breeze for most students, but I couldn't understand simple techniques and couldn't even write my name in first grade. I had to repeat school a couple of times. I repeated grade one twice, grade two twice and form four twice. It's also known as a tenth grade. The usual response would be of despair and hopelessness. My grade one teacher even told my parents that it might be better if they sent me to a school that I could cope with.

Many people didn't think I would get here because along the way I stopped listening to those people. I know you have big dreams. You want to live a more fulfilling life and do more. I know you might struggle with your vision, goals and fears. We all do and what I did wasn't a magic trick. This coming from a person who believed I wouldn't amount to much. I am still learning, but my biggest accomplishment is I refused for anyone to determine my success in life.

If you want to accomplish something you need to start at one end and push over all the obstacles in your path. When you do that it is easier to figure out what the next domino is and this keeps going. That is how the idea for this book was created. I wanted to find a way to create everlasting change.

We all go through moments when we feel like we can't reach the top when we listen to how people see us and what stops us from reaching the top.

**Here is what you will learn in this book:**

**How important it is for your vision to be clear**

**What the 80/20 rule is and how to apply to your life**

**Have strong values**

**Your knowledge, experiences and your why are extremely important**

**How to be more confident**

**How to become more productive**

**What is the law of attraction and why it is important?**

**Keys to success**

**Misconceptions about success**

This book will open your eyes and help you approach things differently. I have managed to pull through many of my hurdles because of the guidelines in this book. This is more than a book about becoming successful. This book is about how to build yourself up from the inside. When you concentrate on internal forces that will change the external, what happens in your life often is a reflection of what you say and believe. If you don't follow through, your life will remain the same.

One of the greatest gifts you can give yourself is taking action. By doing this you are one step closer to making your dreams come true. What is in this book will take time, think of it like riding a bike. When you keep falling, you get up until you can ride the bike.

Everything takes time. It takes time to rewire your brain to think differently and for you to see the world differently.

Each domino in this book has been carefully placed, I wanted to make sure this book was as concise as possible and to put in a few tools that will make the journey to the top a whole lot easier for you. Every chapter you read and understand is another domino that you have pushed back. Keep the momentum and each domino will topple over. I would really love to have the opportunity to hear out your story.

I would really like to know what you think about the book so please could you leave a review telling me in two or three sentences what you thought about it.

# Chapter One

# What is the Domino Effect?

*"The moment you take responsibility for everything in your life is the moment you can change anything in your life." -Hal Elrod*

Here is a  fact.  People don't know how to create everlasting change in their life. They have no idea where to start and how to go from there. It's because society has written everything done for us and told us what we should be expected to do and when.

As a kid, I was obsessed with dominoes. I wanted to understand how one domino tile that falls can cause a ripple effect and make the other domino tiles fall. Most people have come across domino tiles or have played with them.

For the better part of my childhood, I was enamored with the game and at fifteen, it was the first time I heard about the Domino Effect.

.

I wanted to know more about this so I did some digging and what I found out blew my mind. Yeah, the history is a little messed up, but for years people have been using the Domino Effect as a way of achieving success.

I have used the Domino Effect as a way of understanding what I needed to change in my life to get certain results. You are probably thinking how can the Domino Effect help you change your life and how does it involve success. The Compound Effect is similar, it says that for every choice you commit to there will be a ripple effect from that choice.

Even if it is a small decision that you make, there will be a ripple effect from it. And that is why I wrote this book to show you how you can make better choices so that you can change your life and become successful. I figured this out a couple of years ago and my life changed because of the choices I made.

So, yes it is possible for you to change your life and the simplest way to do this is to use the Domino Effect.

In my research, I found out that the Domino Effect has been around since the '50s. At that time many people speculated that if one country fell to communism the other countries would eventually fall. It was why many countries were obsessed with stopping countries from becoming communist. They started calling it the falling domino principle.

A lot has changed since the '80s including the way people live. Nowadays, people desperately want to change and to improve their lifestyles, back in the '50s, people most of the time kept the status quo. Just like how our language has adapted so has the definition of the Domino Effect. It states that when you make a slight change whether in improving your personality or behavior it will then activate a ripple effect and cause a shift in related behaviors.

This may sound nonsensical because as kids we were programmed to believe that a leopard can't change their spots and there were all those kid books that seemed to emphasize that fact. Northwestern University in 2012 did a study and the researchers found out that people who decreased their amount of sedentary leisure time each day, also reduced their daily fat intake. Though the participants weren't asked to reduce their fat intake, they did it because they were spending less time watching TV and eating mindlessly. Because they were active and doing other things the need to eat while watching television wasn't there.

The Domino Effect has everything to do with causation and effect, the occurring events that happen after one main effect. Everything in life is interconnected and so is a success, our habits, human behaviors, and life systems. It's like a chain. When the chain breaks, the beads will fall, one by one. This inherent relatedness is what causes one choice to lead to another choice and for there to be either surprising results that cover all areas of our life. This is one of the reasons the Domino Effect occurs. The other is due to commitment and consistency. Which are the core principles of human behavior? Robert Cialdini explains this phenomenon perfectly in his "Influence" book. If people were to commit and be consistent with an idea or their goals (even in a small way), they are likely to follow with their commitment and accomplish that idea or goal.

## Rules of the Domino Effect

Growing up, the concept of following the rules annoyed the heck out of me. Unless you are a magician and about to pull a rabbit from a hat. Certain rules must be followed, just like there are certain rules meant to be broken. There are guidelines to everything in life and the Domino Effect is no different.

It manifests because of something we put into the works that cause a number of events. Can one event really work in favor of all the other events? It's important to follow these rules in order for the Domino Effect to be effective and get you the desired result that you want in your life.

## Motivation

If you aren't motivated in what you want then chances of the dominoes falling is unlikely. You are far more likely to work on something if you are motivated in achieving it than if you are not motivated at all. If the thought keeps you up at night then that's the area you must focus on.

# Momentum

The reason why locomotives weren't effective was that they had no momentum. It took forever for the train to arrive at the required destination, granted transport in the past wasn't as efficient as it is today, but steam locomotives required too much time and energy than the engine locomotives. In order to get your results and for the Domino Effect to work, you have to work consistently on one goal until it knocks the others in the line. That way, in a short period of time, you get the results you are looking for.

# Progress versus results

What many people get wrong is that they are fixated on getting results before they see progress. They expect that everything will come together before you put the cards together or work in a consistent manner for you to make progress. Think of it this way, in order to be good at a skill like playing guitar, you have to work out the kinks. Practicing is important, even if at the end of the day you still sound like screeching trains on the rails you continue going. You learn how to play the chords before the scales and then once you do that you learn the other tricks like licks and riffs. This is all guitar jargon, but at the end of the day, a beginner guitarist would want to know how to play the riff before the lick and the scales before becoming an advanced guitarist. Progress is crucial in your life, results will come later.

## Where you went wrong

If there is no progress leading up to the next domino whether it be a habit, a rise in your station or a general change in your behavior then you have to go back to brass tactics. Something happened along the way and you have to go back to the three rules to discover what went wrong. The Domino Effect can help you achieve unprecedented results.

How to achieve phenomenal results

## Step One

Follow this book to the tee. Every chapter talks about something critical. That is intentional. Understand the concepts before you proceed to the next chapter. Peter Voogd often says mastery over information overload is extremely important and critical to your success.

## Step Two

Information or instruction without action is like watching a cooking show and never actually cooking what you learned. To grow and adapt you need to follow the action steps that are there. That way you see results. Follow the action steps and in no time your life will change.

## Step Three

Be consistent in everything you do. When you do that you are creating habits that will stay with you even after you have finished this book. Studies say it takes 90 days in order for a new habit to be formed. The unfortunate part is most people don't follow through with a new habit and this pushes them back.

# Chapter Two

# Maximizing the Domino Effect for Your Continued Success

*"The goal in life is not to surpass the expectations we set for ourselves. Success is sweetest when we break our own record, then wake up the next day ready to do it all over again." -Lethia Owens.*

This is the chapter where we dig deeper. Many people think success is hard to attain, but it's because they are looking at it the wrong way.

What at first seems challenging becomes easier but if you keeping doing it then it continues to go like that. That's what is so important about understanding the Domino Effect. After a while of continually doing something it adds up and that's when success is unleashed. But it all starts with the first step. Too often people are too myopic in their views. They think of the now instead of how that will build up and lead to something bigger later on. The big picture is crucial to your understanding of how to get to point B from point A.

## Don't try everything all at once

When I was a little kid I wanted to be on a team. There's something magical about being with a group of people. Just like most kids I then started trying to get into every kind of team at school from tennis to hockey and even soccer. What happened was I eventually wore myself out to the point that I didn't make it into any team.

In chapter one, I pointed out how crucial it is to master something other than overloading yourself with information.

This is the same thing. Don't try to do too many things all at once unless you are planning on getting into the Guinness Book of Records.

Dominoes work the same way. If you have watched dominoes up close, it's quite fascinating. One domino hits the next and that domino hits the other and you know the story. People want to get to the top way too quickly and as a result, they fail, not because they don't have the capacity to do it, but they are doing too much all at once.

The smallest thing that you do such as waking up at 5 am has phenomenal results. You start doing things differently.

It's this reason why people suggest you should wake up early. You have more time to do things that you want to do. You can meditate, pray, read then go jogging and still have time to do other things. You set yourself up for a winning day and when you have a great morning this affects the rest of your day.

In 2012, I was at college in Malaysia. Every night, I would sleep at 9 pm then wake up at 3 am. For thirty minutes, I would meditate and pray. After that, I would listen to the Hour of Power by Tony Robbins. Write in my journal and go to class. I did this for a month because waking up at 3 am is no easy feat, but an amazing thing started to happen to my psyche and my dopamine levels increased exponentially. Everyone thought I had lost my mind, but it's all to do with psychology. The start of our day is very important.

This is a minor example of how powerful it is to tackle one thing because that leads to you scoring a bigger goal than you could have imagined. It applies to everything in life including health, job, family, and lifestyle. Doing one thing well spreads like a wildfire to all areas of our life and before you know it your life will be exactly how you imagined it to be.

## The 80/20 Rule

Remember as kids being barraged about working so hard that we became exhausted and started seeing stars. That's the only way to get success right, by being so overwhelmed that we would be bedridden for days. It's a principle that has been there for so long, it's ingrained in our minds. Work extremely hard, then you will see the desired results. It might have worked back in the day or before the rise in innovations and technology.

This is why so many people are hesitant about success, they see it as an esoteric quality only a few can achieve and the term work smart and not hard doesn't register. Success is for anyone who knows how to work the system and understands the rules that apply to it.

The 80/20 rule is so powerful because it incorporates all that. Sometimes it's called the principle of factor sparsity, the law of the vital few and more commonly the Pareto Principle.

This principle was first suggested by management thinker Joseph M. Juran who named it after Italian economist Vilfredo Pareto who noted the 80/20 connection while at the University of Lausanne in 1896. He had stated in his book "Cours d'economie Politique," that only 80% of Italy's wealth belonged to 20% of the population. Since then the principle has been used in economics, science, business, software, and sports. Now it states that 80% of effects from events come from 20% of the causes. Another definition for it is 20% of the effort will give you 80% of the results.

You probably are scratching your head and wondering what this has to do with the domino effect or even success. How much effort does it take for one domino to fall? Not a lot. That one push causes a chain reaction of similar events that leads you to achieve ultimate success. It might not make a lot of sense, but it gives me some time to explain its significance to our lives.

I came across this principle in 2015, I didn't really understand it. Many people swore by this exact principle, then I watched a video explaining this principle. I watched a Jeff Goins webinar where he was talking about this principle and how to apply it to your life. We are all passionate about certain things like for example arts and crafts. If you are passionate, then you tend to be good. Chances are you will spend about 20% of your efforts and that gives you 80% of the results.

The outcome can come in different ways from success, praise, appreciation or even monetary value, but if you aren't passionate, the results are completely different.

The Pareto principle and Domino Effect work hand in hand. It takes you 20% of your efforts to push one domino down and that, in turn, will result in that domino pushing the next. This is where 80% of your outcomes take place. One tiny action leads to insurmountable results. Monetary gain is the end result of all the fallen dominoes, it's the very last domino that is harder to push down than the other dominoes. Once it has fallen, you would have accomplished the Pareto Principle and the Domino Effect.

Think of it like this. Chandler Bolt, a bestselling author wrote his first book at twenty-years-old. He published The Productive Person on Amazon and he had no experience with writing books. He put in 20% of the effort and his outcome was 80%. Since then he has built a business called the self-publishing school. He also continues to make mass amounts of profit from his books which include Published and Book Launch.

Another example is Daniel Dipiazza who at twenty-four decided he wanted to change his life. He went to a site called Elance where he offered to design people's websites for a particular price. After four months, he had over $24 000 and built a site called Rich 20 Something. That one action led him to produce massive results.

There are many examples out there of people who only put 20% of their effort and received 80% of the benefits. I'm by no means promoting people to become sloths or unproductive, 20% may not seem like a lot, but it actually is.

People need to start working smart because over-exerting yourself doesn't necessarily mean that the results you come up with will have the desired effect. If you push a domino too hard then what will happen is that the domino line becomes haphazard and some of the dominoes fly out of reach.

## Applying the Domino Effect with the Pareto Principle

For any principle to work, you have to allow the process to do the work. In order for this to work you have to look at your life and decide what domino you need to topple over first. There are of course steps that lead to success.

Wherever you are in life, your experiences, upbringing, and surroundings define every moment of your life. They define what's important to you, the gifts you have, your purpose, where you would want to be in the next 12 months and lastly, they have molded you to this point in time. The examples I gave about the people who became successful even though they had nothing going for them have proven success is achievable.

In life, we all go through barriers and walls that stop us from performing at the stage we are supposed to and that's why the Domino Effect works. It's like a carpenter who scraps away from the outer layers of wood. He saws and designs until it forms a shape.

Success will not wait for you, it will not be gentle with you because if you want to leave behind a legacy, change the world and become the best version of yourself then you first need to mold yourself.

It's mandatory that you scrap away the bad bits, push down the walls and mold yourself to create exceptional results. Ultimately, if you desire that the last domino in the stack to fall down then you need to slowly get to the position where that is possible.

# Your Values Define Your Success

*"Begin each day with the blueprint of my deepest values firmly in the mind. Then when challenges come, make decisions based on those values." -Stephen Covey*

Everyone knows what values are and what they represent.

The dictionary defines it as the regard that something is held to deserve, the importance, worth or usefulness of something. Another definition is that there are principles or standards of behavior, one's judgment of what's important in life.

Basically, values are what we think are important, our beliefs, opinions, tastes, and preferences.

People underestimate how powerful our values are. They determine so much of our lives and push us on a the journey that has been predestined from the beginning. When we are children we are so enamored with the world. Everything sparks our interest and the adults around us have formed their values already. Our brains haven't finished forming to the point we can make up our mind, so when someone points out something, we follow through with that idea.

From an early stage, our values are formed from those around us and this continues to adulthood. It's why there are so many cases of people who grow up to be abusive just like their parents because those were the values they grew up with. Values are so important because they determine the direction we go on and the choices we make.

Our values are part of our belief system and it is important to fully understand what that itself represents.

I grew up in a family of three. My family is extremely artistic and sporty. Every weekend my parents and brother would go and play tennis. When it came to the arts, my father could draw a life-like lion. My brother was great at drawing comic book characters, my mother at maps and my sister could paint, draw and sing. It was my belief that to be part of that family I had to be like them; to be a great artist or to play some kind of sport. My brother could play tennis and basketball so I tried my luck with both. My sister was the goalkeeper in her hockey team, captain of the basketball team; she played tennis for fun and swam for her school.

For the longest time, I sought to be just like them, to have their views and opinions. To hold sport and art in a high light. When it came down to it, my values were aligned with their values because I thought they had to be.

The first domino to tackle is our values and discover what your values are and not the ones you latched onto because you believed you had to. Most people don't know what their values are and their opinions are formed from the opinions of others.

The reason I put the value as the first domino is that it's so important for you to understand what they are. Values are the reasons why someone chooses one country to live in over the other or chooses a certain career and if they aren't clear it's hard to figure out where to go next.

People who value health become health conscious and exercise daily, eat the right foods. Those who value honesty work at it and are the most honest people. People who value loyalty, look for this quality in their friends and are extremely loyal. They don't gossip and never stab their friends in the back.

Many who value helping others are altruistic and dedicate their lives to making the people around them comfortable. These are people who are social workers, teachers and work in charities or are missionaries. How do we change our values so that they become so powerful it creates a ripple effect?

## Raise Your Standards

The first thing about changing your life is to raise your standards. Basically, raise your values, want more and change the way you look at the world. If you value honesty, make sure you live a completely honest life. If you value success, work hard at attaining it by ensuring that you are morally incorruptible, honest and develop yourself constantly. Every successful person has to raise their standards, constantly work at figuring themselves out and read any book that will give them the chance to do that.

## Stop the Limiting Beliefs

Far too many people have limiting beliefs and that's because they don't value themselves as much as they think they do. I remember being eighteen and thinking I didn't amount to anything. I saw myself disappearing into oblivion. I didn't value myself. Because of that, I doubted myself, didn't make an effort to be anything more than I thought I could be. Whenever I got a compliment I thought the person was lying to me.

Limiting beliefs affect us in more ways. They dictate how we spend the days as the words bite our flesh and cause us to be afflicted. These beliefs all start from the root and that's our values, they manifest in so many ways and our dreams are washed away because of that.

If you want to be successful in anything (and I'm not just talking about financial freedom, but also mentally free), you need to stop the hindrances that are coming from you. That's right, the only one stopping you from achieving what you are meant to achieve is you and not the man in the mirror.

The problem lies with the way our generation grew up. It grew up in a time of video vixens who looked far too beautiful to be real. A time when so many young stars emerged out of the woodwork. Nowadays, there are far too many young stars under forty and below who are millionaires. So, it's easy for there to be too many limiting beliefs. In a world with so much static, it's easier to see yourself as someone who can't amount to much.

## Your passions will ignite your values

When you close your eyes, what is the first thing you think about? When you wake up, what is the first thing that pops in your head? Have you ever read the book "Letters To A Young Poet" by Rainer Maria Rilke? In the book, a poet writes to someone who's esteemed and in the profession, the writer wants to get into. There's one quote in the book that's extremely powerful, "If, when you wake up in the morning, you can think of nothing but writing…then you are a writer."

This holds true to every part of our lives and we just don't know it. Our passions are right there, but because we haven't spent time reflecting on them, we follow what everyone wants us to do. You might be great at numbers and because of that you did something that has to do with numbers, but that might not be your passion or what you want to do with the rest of your life.

Let's push passions aside and focus on what motivates you. Motivation is defined as the reasons for doing something or your behavior. What motivates you can either strengthen you or break you. If your motivation is money then the problem with that is you will never be satisfied and you will do anything to get it. Now, success is the exact opposite. It is the accomplishment of an aim or purpose and it can affect every area. Success is based on the principle that if you work hard in one area, it will resonate with every part of you and it will affect all other areas.

## Understanding your worth

Your values only become stronger if you understand your worth. In Grant Cardone's book "The 10X Rule," he talks about the importance of how success is your responsibility, duty, and obligation to yourself and your family.

There's an immense power behind self-belief and valuing yourself and your values. You can change the world because you believe you can, you know your limits and what motivates you. There are too many people out there who don't value themselves enough and their capabilities. Because of that, they never go anywhere. The power to be all you want to be is within you. All you need to do is understand that and accept it.

This is the very first domino that must be pushed because without values you are likely never to know what you really want to do.

# The Importance of Clarity

*"Simplicity, clarity, singleness: these are attributes that give our lives power and vividness and joy." Richard Halloway*

I remember being eight-years-old and having a dream with my childhood friend. My dream was to change the world whether it was through acting, music or being the president of the United States. By the way, I'm not an American, but for a little kid, I thought it was possible and spent time

crafting how I would do it.

In the fifth grade, the classes combined and the teachers sat us down and asked what we wanted to become. I had told no one about my dream to be the president and all the kids said the normal kind of dreams nine to ten-year-old kids have. Which usually involves being athletes, tennis players, firemen and famous. My childhood friend, Martha and I were the enigmas in the group and that made us strong. We had a strong desire to be more than our circumstances. She wanted to be a doctor.

My turn came after about twenty kids and I took a deep breath. I had thought about this exact moment for a week and knew without a doubt what I wanted to be.

Martha's teacher asked, "What do you want to be when you grow up?"

My chest puffed out and I said. "I want to be the president of the United States."

You can guess the response was mixed some of the kids looked like I had stolen their dessert and the teachers stared at me as though I lost my mind.

Martha's teacher was perplexed and asked me again. "I beg your pardon, I don't think I heard you correctly."

I knew people would think me mad, I knew they would think I was delusional, but I knew one person would not see me that way and that's all that mattered. My parents and siblings wouldn't understand, but Martha would. It gave me enough courage to say it again.

"I want to be president of the United States of America."

This time the kids laughed, but unashamedly I didn't care. It was my dream and no one could steal that from me and not even the satisfaction of knowing it would be fulfilled. The teachers scratched their heads.

"Why not the president of Zimbabwe?" One of them asked.

I pondered the question. "Because that won't make a difference. If I want to change Zimbabwe then that would make sense, but America is the most powerful country in the world. And I want to change the world."

Another teacher asked. "But you could be the first female president and that would change the world."

I shook my head. I was relentless and I said more confidently. "I want to do more than change the world. I want to impact it across the world and not in one country."

Granted, my dream was a bit too ambitious, considering to be qualified, I had to first be an American, but it didn't matter that I wasn't. I would get to the White House sooner or later. I was a weird kid and that's the best explanation I can give.

For a little kid who didn't fully grasp how the world was, I knew I wanted to be more and change the world. To climb mountains many people saw were too high, to me, it didn't matter how many hurdles I would jump, I would.

## How Powerful Clarity Is

As time went on my dream changed and so did I. I knew I could help the world even if I didn't get to the white house. I had more to offer and I worked on that by understanding who I was and what I wanted from life. At thirteen I discovered writing.

Our gifts come when we least expect it. For me, I was a boarder and since I was so used to killing my brain cells by watching too much television I was bored. So, I took out a thin book and I started writing. I just wrote. My first story was about five super kids and it was more like a rip-off from Power Rangers, but I didn't care. It was the one hint I had gotten in terms of where I wanted to go. At that point in time, I wanted to be an actor and singer. It was my belief I could help the world through that, but when I wrote in that book my dream took a different form. It changed me, I believed for the first time in my life I had potential.

I used to believe I wasn't particularly bright. I had intelligent friends like Martha who could calculate large numbers all in her head. Anastasia and Letso were brilliant at writing. So, to discover something like this blew my mind. It was my first aha moment. Blame it on me being a late bloomer, but for me, I saw my whole life shift in a different direction and this was it. The point in my life where things would be different.

Being thirteen is confusing enough without having to add in a new talent I never thought I had, for that whole year I wrote short stories in a hard-covered book and showed people who thought I had copied the stories. It didn't matter that they didn't believe me, I knew one day I would be a writer and that was where I could go.

The funny thing is, I ha reading. Now, I don't. Then I had to wrestle with my family when it came to reading. I didn't like staring long at the tiny words in a book that had no relevance to what I was going through. I also detested it because I struggled with concentration. For me to want to become a writer was like someone who never liked music saying they wanted to be a musician.

The problem was I knew what I wanted to become, but I wasn't clear about it. I had no idea when it would be, how my life would be like in a few years or how many books I would have written. I didn't even understand the law of writing, neither did I even understand what it truly means to be a writer. My vision or dream wasn't clear.

It was so unclear that I stopped writing from the time I was fourteen to seventeen. I showed my high school friends Makenna and PJ my book and they gave me nothing, but support, but I was so unsure of myself that I vowed not to show anyone my work again.

Here and there, I broke the rule. When people said they read better I believed it because I had lost what I had at ten. This relentless belief in my dream, vision and who I was.

When you are clear with your dream, no one can tell you otherwise. You believe in it so much that you would do anything to make it a reality and that makes all the difference in life. The clearer you are the more real it is. Many people think all you need is a vision, but the reality of the situation is a vision will only take you so far if you aren't clear about it.

Napoleon Hill spoke fervently about clarity in "Think and Grow Rich," you could say he was an advocate on the topic. He studied the habits and traits of successful people and found that they all had clear dreams. They knew how they would get to the different levels in their journey and that made their dream even more powerful.

## How Clarity Shapes Your Life

The great thing about clarity is it gives you purpose. It is the gear in a machine that moves and continues to move so you get to your destination. Many people believe they can go through life without being clear about what they want.

The problem with that is it's so easy for you to get distracted along the course and choose a different route. When we were kids, we had dreams and they do change, but there was always a link somewhere down the line and all we needed to do was be willing to find it.

Let's take Jessica Scorpio for example. She was attending Singularity University in 2012, the co-founder of Google asked a classroom of 40 students to pick one idea that could impact a billion people. Jessica knew she wanted to change the world with one idea and she formulated a plan. What she wanted was to do a car service. There are thousands of car services around the world, but the difference is this car service would involve people sharing their cars with their neighbors. It's almost like Uber, the difference is her car service is about connecting people in the same area and building relationships with those people.

Jonas Falk saw that there was a problem with the school system in America, the food was unhealthy and if it was healthy it didn't taste great. He came up with an idea to distribute healthy food and though he was competing against long-established companies, that didn't deter him.

His three key principles were to serve healthy food, provide great service and make people happy.

Sangu Delle, a Ghanaian entrepreneur created Golden Palm Investments. He saw that there was a deficit when it came to investing in real estate, agribusiness and technology especially if it was in the early stages. He wanted to solve that problem by creating a company that did that and also invested in growth capital. More than anything, Sangu wanted to bring significant changes to Africa.

The link here is they all had one idea, one main cause and they linked that idea with a plan on how to achieve it. They made sure their ideas were clear. Many successful people want to change the world. They want to impact their community and that one cause gives them drive. But can you imagine if they had no concrete plan on how to do it? You need to know what you want and how you going to get there. Winging it won't cut it especially when you are playing with top-level players.

*Chapter Five*

# Have a Vision

*"Vision without action is merely a dream. Action without vision just passes the time. Vision with action can change the world." -Joel A. Barker*

**W**hen you are clear with what you want in life, a vision is formed and with that vision, you have a better understanding of who you are and what you want.

I often told my father visionaries are what change the world and it's true because all the greats were visionaries Thomas Edison, Bill Gates, Ophrah Winfrey, Steve Jobs, Dr. Shirley Ann Jackson, and Madam C. J. Walker.

Vision is defined by the dictionary as the faculty of being able to see or the ability to think about or plan the future with imagination and wisdom.

I used to be friends with this girl. From the time we started talking, she would talk about her love for food. Her eyes brightened at the mention of dishes I never heard about, her posture relaxing when she imagined going home and cooking those extravagant meals. Even though she was having problems at home, you could tell that cooking for her was a release and what she wanted more than anything was to cook She often spoke of the restaurant she would open and the name it would have. We were seventeen-year-old kids and here she had a clear vision of what she wanted for her life. Storms brewed around her, money was hard to come by and yet she pushed forward. I didn't understand where the fervor was coming from because if I had been in her situation, it would be an entirely different story.

Her parents weren't around, her sister seemed not to care as much as she was supposed to. Some days she didn't know where she would get money to pay for her groceries. Other days, she had no problems at all. But she made it work. There was a time she spoke to me about going overseas to learn culinary arts, but even though that didn't happen, she worked with what she had. She focused her energy on cooking and her world changed. Now, she has opened a restaurant. Her vision didn't disappear when problems came rushing at her. She didn't stop to catch her breath or complain that she couldn't possibly achieve her dreams with her problems.

Here's another example of a strong vision. In 2014, I went to South Africa and lived there for six months. I met this young woman who changed my life. Juliette Bush is one of the most unique individuals I have come across. She has unwavering faith and inner beauty. When I met her, she was blogging and told me she was writing a book. It was a nonfiction book on her life and I was blown away that here was someone writing a book.

You would be shocked at how many people write books, but actually, don't publish them. I've come across quite a number who say they will publish but end up not. I can't say whether it's because their vision wasn't strong enough or maybe they got terrified of the prospect of writing a book. No genre is more intimate, truthful and honest as a non-fiction book.

I watched Juliette create a website called Brave by Faith. She interviewed many people from across the world about their faith journeys and I was moved again by the progress she was making. This woman had the vision to travel the world and show people God's love and she was the embodiment of all that. Then in 2016, I was blown away again when she published her book Brave by Faith. Here was this woman who had a vision and had accomplished her vision in less than two years. It probably was a long journey and I was seeing the fruits of her belief and faith.

Here are two different individuals, one a Zimbabwean and the other an American. All had the vision to follow their dreams and be more than just ordinary.

## Who Do You Want to Be?

As I said before dreams change, but take up a different form. It's our duty to understand what that new form is, adapt to the changes and figure out what to do next.

The question here is who do you want to be? I've wanted to be a writer since I was thirteen. Visions are extremely powerful, but many don't follow that vision because of fear. They fear what people might say or whether they will fail. That's normal. It's an absolutely normal reaction. We all want to be accepted; to be like cheerleaders who follow the norm and not go against the current.

Your vision is what defines you and pushes you in the right direction. People without a vision are aimless, they jump from one job to the next and are never satisfied with what they have. Those without a clear vision tend to pass time. They are also frustrated with themselves and life because they have this passion that isn't being fueled. There's nothing worse than going through life knowing your purpose, but not following through it.

It's a depressing state that can go on until you figure out who you want to be. The question was easier as little kids when our dreams were bigger than our circumstances and anything was possible. Nothing could get in our way.

Time is often like that. And the problem with society is, we are so accustomed to telling people what they can't do instead of what they can do. The Wright Brothers went through it. So did Katherine G. Johnson. The fault lies in the human mindset where it's hard to process certain things like a portable radio, watching pictures on the television, or even cars that move by themselves instead of using horses. Where would we be without Henry Ford?

Your dream might have appeared too big as a kid and because of that many squashed it until it was like bubblegum sticking to your heels. Always there, but no one saw how it was pulling you back. That's how powerful a vision is. The voices, of course, stopped you from pursuing that vision no matter how ridiculous it might have seen or appeared.

## The Link Between Clarity and Vision

Whatever you do in life, the stronger your vision is the more undeterred you are in accomplishing it. The voices become nothing more than murmurs as you strive to achieve what many deemed impossible.

I have come across such voices in my life. I was born with ADHD but only found out in my early twenties. Even though I had no name for it, I knew something was wrong somewhere. I found it hard to focus, pay attention and even understand what most people were talking about. It took twice as long to understand a new concept unlike everyone else who understood it right away. Focusing in class, was hard so instead, I dreamed about a better life and often got reprimanded for not paying attention.

Failing was a normal routine for me. I didn't enjoy school and the thought of going to a class where I had to spend time trying to get concepts I didn't understand was hard. If it wasn't for Martha, it would have been a lot harder for me, but it was more bearable.

The teachers thought I would amount to nothing and that didn't change even when I went to high school. Many of the teachers thought I should drop out and attend a school better fitted to my standards. There was a time in high school when I believed I could be more. I failed and had to repeat the year. My confidence was shaken.

The one subject I was good at was English and my confidence in it improved when I went from one school to the next. A lot of people didn't think I would go to university, let alone graduate and I believed they were right until I refused that for my life.

One way or the other I was going to university. My vision was to graduate with high scores and to prove all those who thought I wouldn't amount to anything wrong.

My friends along the journey helped me out. My childhood friends stood by my side; my close friend from the first high school I attended pointed out I had more in me than I believed I did.

Though there are negative voices that push your vision back, there are also those that fuel the vision to become a bright flame. The problem is we tend to listen to the negativity more due to the doubt that constantly floods our minds. I listened to the negative voices for so long, but I realized I wanted to prove I could do it. And I did.

I went to Malaysia then Switzerland where I did a six-month bulk education program, I knew I wanted to be in the Upper Second Class. I didn't know how I was going to achieve that because I had come late to school because of visa problems and everyone was way ahead of me.

For four months, I struggled with class. The year prior to that I had been at home because we couldn't raise the hefty twenty-four thousand school fees, but regardless of that, I was at school. I made it.

When your vision is strong and clear even if it's something like graduating with an upper second it will happen because you believe it and work on it. Everything aligns with your vision, the creator will make sure it comes to fruition. You focus on it and you will be rewarded for it.

What I have learned is never to put limits on visions, it's as big and small as you want it to be. But if you want to make a difference then you have to have a big vision because you will see significant changes in your life when you do just that.

# Chapter Six

# The Link Between Your Past, Present, and Future

*"Only as high as I reach can I grow, only as far as I seek can I go, only as deep as I look can I see, only as much as I dream can I be." Karen Raun*

Do you often ignore the clues from your past because it's easier to do so? The past is ridden with so many cues, but because of how hectic our lives have gotten, the past is like a page ripped out of a very old book.

Your purpose or your why is written in the cues of the past. Everything you know has led you to this very moment. This is the part of the book where we get deep down and discover how to mold you. This is the hardest domino you have to push down because of all the hurt and pain that's laid on top.

Thinking about the past is hard, your failures, the people who left and the discouragement you faced. But if you want to go forward, you have to push aside each brick that's laced with fear, dread, anger, loss and hurt. Pick up the bricks and throw them until they become nothing more than debris. You need to let go and what you will discover is that the past has a clue that will lead you to your why.

When I was sixteen it was one of the most difficult times. Being sixteen for most people is. It's a time when you have to figure things out and decide what you want. There are so many inside and outside forces that you can't seem to control, from raging hormones to doubt that keeps creeping up. Then there's the phase of wondering if what you look like is good enough. For me being seventeen involved all that and having to deal with low grades, wondering what my parents would think and being sick.

At the beginning of the year, I got ulcers, so it made life a whole lot difficult for me, I was constantly sick and concentrating was hard. For a while, I had to take medication so the open sores in my duodenum would heal. The year didn't let up. I got better, but one of my closest friends got sick. Being a border was one of the most eye-opening experiences I have ever been through.

In my stream, we were all like a close-knit family and when one of my friends got sick, it affected all twenty-two of the girls.

She went home and came back to write her exams, but she got sick again and they had to pull her out. These exams were one of the most important exams anyone could write in my country. It dictated whether someone could go to the next grade or if they had to be held back. I was worried. Two weeks passed and she still hadn't come back to write any of the exams. On the last day, I heard she was writing at home. Relief poured in me and I relaxed.

On the last day of exams, we packed our suitcases and went back home. For a few weeks, I felt a sense of pride and happiness. Dread filled me that I didn't pass, but I did my best to ignore it. My sister came back from being at college in Australia. It was the 30th of November 2007. Nearly ten years ago. I was excited to have her back, she was my right-wing and the person I counted on the most. After Martha had left to go to England, my sister became the person I relied on the most.

That day I felt off though. There was a numbing feeling I couldn't shake and my head wasn't in it. I didn't know what was wrong, but I knew something was. After the ritual of presents which I always looked forward to. My parents left. I can't remember where they disappeared, but when they had gone I went into my room. Back then I had a pink Motorolla phone, even though it couldn't store music, I loved it to bits.

I picked up the phone and I received a message from one of my friends, who was a stream below me. In the message, she wrote the words, "I'm sorry your friend died."

At that moment, everything seemed to stop and the world halted for a bit. My sixteen-year-old friend who was the most beautiful soul I had ever met was dead. I remembered how she always encouraged me when I doubted myself. She believed in me more than I believed in myself. Tatenda had this light very few people possess and all the memories with her in it started to catch up to me.

I realized in that very moment how short life is.

## Your Knowledge

Every day we learn something new one way or the other, either by reading about it or watching it.

The powerful thing with knowledge is it guides us in the direction we want to go to. Maybe it's a new cause that has been highlighted and it gets you excited. It could motivate you to understand the world better. Learning never stops and the more you learn, the more it fills you up. This is the key to growing up. There's a huge difference between being sixteen, seventeen, twenty-one, twenty-two and it goes on. Each year, you are older, bolder and more invested into shaping your life.

It's assumed that because you might not be a brain box that you don't have the knowledge to teach people, but that's a misconception. Who you are today is because of years of learning that has been going on in the background from the conversations you had to the books you read. And as your knowledge grows so does your insight into who you are and where you would like to go.

## Your Experiences

What have you been through that has shaped who you are today? Experiences affect us in more ways than you would think. As kids, we saw certain things such as our friends being bullies, two things could have happened. You might have become a bully or advocated against it.

People who go through being cyberbullied end up advocating against it. Every experience has some form of repercussion, from becoming overweight to anorexic. They all link to a momentous event in your life that pushed you into a certain direction.

Adam Braun went on a trip called a Semester at Sea, he went to different countries and realized many kids didn't have pencils. It was then that Adam realized how difficult it was to get a pencil in developing countries. It was that one moment that made him want to start a charity organization and he did. He started Pencils of Promise.

Ashley Zahabian was an overweight teenager who kept going to the hospital and she disliked being that overweight kid. Her experiences of being tormented, depressed and loathing every moment of it made her want to change her life around. She started caring about what she ate, exercised daily and decided she wanted more out of life. At just seventeen she became a motivational speaker, but if she hadn't had those experiences then she wouldn't be who she is today.

These experiences cultivated these people to change their course and discover what they really wanted. One momentous experience can change your life in so many ways if you allow it.

It can fuel your passion, your desire, that thump in your chest, but only if you look at your experiences. There's an untold story, a way to change the world and it's waiting for you to use it to take charge of your life.

## Your Why

For you to make a difference in your life, you need to have a why. A reason you want to change the world. Mine, if I'm being honest, was Tatenda's death. Sure, I had passion, drive, and determination. I wanted to change the world, but before that moment, it wasn't as strong as it is now.

I had become lazy with my plans. I kept relying on life happening to me instead of me taking the chance to do something. Remember this quote:

"Life doesn't happen to you, it happens because of you."

I thought that one day I would have that aha or eureka moment and everything would be clear, but I wasn't doing anything to change that. It took the death of my friend to realize I owed her. I can't explain it, but she had so much faith in me and that thought remains with me today.

The question you should ask yourself is what is your why. The reason you wake up every day or do you just pass life by thinking that things will align for you. They never will. You will keep waiting and keep hoping, but until you take charge, your life will remain the same.

I'm a strong advocate for how short life is. Simply because I have seen far too many young people die because of foolishness or illness. The way I see it, is you have one life and a couple of chances for you to change the world. When you die, what will you be remembered for? It's not about how much money you make, but your impact on the world. Did your story help a kid who went through bullying? Did your story help a college dropout who believed they were worthless? What are you living for?

It's a scary thought to go out there, but if you know that it's going to help someone out, then that makes all the difference. Let your voice help those who need to hear it so they know they aren't the only ones going through this.

## The Link

Your knowledge, experiences and your why will shape you. Allow them to. The past, present, and future are all linked by the above three. There's so much power in them, but we at times don't fully utilize what we have.

The past is full of experiences waiting for you to use them to change the world. Those experiences shape your present and this leads you to the future. In a few years, what do you want people to say you stand for? How do you want to change or impact it?

There are moments in the past full of many painful memories.

For so long, the past dictated my present until I let go of the pain. There was nothing I could have done to stop any of it and I had to let that sink in to move on. It doesn't mean that I don't think of the past and link it to my present. I look back, not with despondency, but with a sense of gratitude that all those moments cultivated me. They made me stronger and made me who I am today.

As you go forward, understand that the past mistakes and failures don't define you, instead they build you up. They bring you up because regardless of all those mistakes, they have made you into who you are today.

# Chapter Seven

# Taking Confidence by the hand

*Be humble in your confidence yet courageous in your character." -Melanie Koulouris*

Confidence is one of those rare gifts so hard to get a hold of. One moment it's there and the next it's gone like it was never there, to begin with. When that happens, it's as though we feel like we're lacking on some grounds. Kids are so confident, they say what they want without thinking twice about it, they move like nothing can stop them from going forward.

Kids run around and don't think about how they might get hurt in the process. They play with anyone who wants to play with them. They are full of so much energy and excitement.

Confidence is not as hard as people think it is because there's a reason as to why you aren't as confident as you were. It could be as a kid you were ridiculed. We all go through it, the dreadful moment when we realize we might be a bit strange and it affects us especially in primary to high school. All we really want is to be accepted. So many people long to know they belong and when they feel like they don't, their confidence is shattered. Their world is thrown into a loophole as they discover people don't see them in the proper light.

I have been to nine schools. In first grade, I was unstoppable because I was the teacher's pet. I left that school to go to another where I met Martha. The feeling of being unstoppable didn't dim, I was surrounded by awesome people. The third primary school I went to, things started to change. The popular kids teased me, they acted as though I was stupid and my confidence started to dim. It had been a challenge for me to go to that school. I wanted to go because Martha was there and to me, I would jump every hurdle to go where she was.

I lost a bit of my confidence. My back started slumping and I bowed my head where I went, I thought I wasn't worth anything and it all goes back to being in primary school. It also has to do with me failing seventh grade and it being difficult in getting into a private high school.

There are so many factors that mess up our confidence and by reflecting on them you can build up yourself back up.

## Three Common Factors That Affect Your

# Confidence

There are far more than three, but everyone grapples with rejection, failure, and self-doubt. It's the underlining factor that pushes us back and makes us not want to pursue our dreams.

# Rejection

How many times have you been rejected by society or the world? How many times have people laughing at you? What about that job you wanted but you didn't get it? Rejection is part of the new normal. A lot of people have a hard time dealing with it and that's absolutely normal. People avoid going all out because of fear of rejection. One thing I have come to realize is that people are bound to reject your values, beliefs, dreams, and plans if it doesn't fit well into their plans.

Not getting that job doesn't mean you aren't capable, but the job might not be the right one for you. The creator's plans for you are bigger than the plans you have for yourself. Whatever you believe in, rejection isn't there to define who you are, but to push you outside of your comfort zones.

# Failure

Failure should never be seen as a low point in your life. It should strengthen you. I have had to repeat three times, it can be depressing failing. Failure is the push you need. It will make you revalue yourself time and time again. But you will be much stronger because of it. If Thomas Edison had not failed a thousand times, he would have not created the light bulb. He kept pushing despite the obstacles laid before him and they were many. He didn't give up.

# Self-doubt

We are own worst enemy. Not your co-worker, boss, colleagues or neighbors. Words are a powerful tool, so powerful that it makes us feel insecure and want to hide under a rug, but words can only hurt you if you allow them too.

We have grown up in a world where we are meant to accept the status quo. We are meant to accept that life is the way it is and not to do anything about it. The school system teaches us to go through the worn path of getting an education, graduating, getting a job and the list goes on. The same applies to words when someone tells us something, we are meant to take it as the truth. How people see you is their truth and not yours.

Once you start listening to people's negativity, all it does it keep you from going after your dreams. You see yourself the way they see you and the words never seem to go away. They keep playing over and over again. Our brain is wired in the same way a computer is. Code is programmed into a computer and if that code repeats then it becomes part of how the computer operates.

Our brain is the same way. At first, you don't believe the lie then you start to because of other circumstances. Self-doubt is vicious and it can destroy your life. There are so many stories of people who doubted themselves and lived a life that they had never wished for. If any new opportunity comes your way and you may hesitate because of fear of failing then doubt has intercepted.

Sure, everyone has their doubts, even Steven Spielberg and J. K Rowling have grappled with it. If you aren't following your dreams because of doubt then you are allowing it to dictate your life and what you can offer the world.

# Proven Ways To Boost Your Self-Confidence

If 2017 is going to be the year you change your life then you can't do it without confidence. This is a critical step to knocking off the last domino and you need to build yourself. Will it be hard? Everything at first starts that way, but with these few steps, you can be on your way to moving closer to your goals.

## Nothing but positive thoughts

We truly are our own worst enemies. Do you take note of the number of negative thoughts toward yourself? Are you being accountable and declaring that you won't allow doubt, negativity, and insecurities to cloud your vision and stop you from achieving your goals. If you want to go anywhere in life you must first believe it with all your heart.

## Believe in yourself and your dreams

My brother had this big board with a poem and on top, it was written the Winner's Creed. I used to love going into his bedroom just to stare at the words because they gave me a taste of confidence, but I never truly understood the words until I was much older.

*"If you think you are beaten then you are. If you think you dare not, you don't. If you think you will lose then you have lost. If you think you would like to win but think you can't. It's almost certain you won't. Success begins with one's will. It's all in the state of mind."*

This is the condensed version of the poem, but the point is succinct. Our thoughts dictate where we are going to go and who we are going to be. You must have a strong belief in who you are and your dreams because until you believe in your dreams no one else will. And until you push for them, no one else will. More importantly, you have to want it.

## Know yourself

A lot of people have no idea who they are and that's why they lack confidence. I'm not talking about simple details like your history, favorite food, and hobbies. I'm talking your truth, values, the negative thoughts that inhibit you, why you haven't achieved your dreams and what's holding you back.

What's your truth? If someone was to interview you and ask you tough questions about your positive traits, what you want to achieve, what are your limitations and capabilities? Would you be able to answer the questions?

To know yourself you need to dig deep and that involves a lot of tissues, so many people brush that aside. But there are vast benefits to knowing who you are, that way no one can tell you who they think you are.

## Past Achievements

It is far too easy to bash ourselves over what we haven't done or achieved. We look at what we failed at and this lowers our self-esteem. Everyone is in a rush to get somewhere that they forget what they learned or gained on the journey to get there. It is crucial for you to see your achievements as an opportunity for more success and more gains and not losses.

## Don't let people define you

A lot of people get caught in the never-ending pool of caring what people think. It becomes like an itch you can't scratch and when it starts, it's hard to ignore. People will have their opinions no matter what. If they see you doing something they don't understand, they call you lazy. If you are busy working on a passion project then they call you distracted and a workaholic.

No matter what you do, people will always have opinions. Caring what people think will drive you insane. It's a waste of time and energy to be worried about what people think of you. Don't let them define you. Understand who you are and what you stand for, everything else is just static and won't get you to where you want to be.

## Accept that you are a work in progress

This statement encompasses so many things, but the one thing that stands out is you don't have to be perfect. You don't have to be a perfect daughter, son, friend, wife or husband.

At times, it's easier to be critical of our mistakes and by doing that, we tend to be brutal. What this does, in turn, is you never understand all the blessings, opportunities and victories around you. We are all work in progress. We make mistakes and often we do things that can be considered stupid. If you are too harsh on yourself then that will decrease your self-esteem. It won't help you at all if all you do is focus on what you haven't accomplished. Understand that on this journey you will make many mistakes.

## Putting It All Together

There are many ways you can boost your self-esteem and become more confident you, but the ones listed above will deliver the best results. Confidence is a science and figuring out the tricks to achieving it makes all the difference.

If you want to be confident then you need to take the necessary measures to make sure you become confident. Know that you have done so much, celebrate your victories, ignore those who have nothing, but negative comments and understand that you are a work in progress. Going forward in life, if you are going to achieve your dreams then you must first understand who you are and that no one can stop you besides yourself.

# The Law of Attraction

*"Whatever you think and talk about paves the runaway
for what you will create." Alan Cohen*

This law has been around for so many years and became

a key factor to success when the book "The Secret" by Rhonda Byrne came out. Many see this idea of attracting things into being as mysticism. It depends on the way you look at it, but the law of attraction isn't a magical word. It's scientific and affects our lives more than we like to admit.

So what is the law of attraction? Simply put, the law of attraction means that we are responsible for bringing in negative and positive forces into our life.

No, you aren't jinxed. You think you are jinxed and that's why often, at times, things don't seem to work out. Believe it or not, I used to be so superstitious to the point where I was looking for three-leafed clovers in my mom's garden. This superstitious nature started from watching an episode of Johnny Bravo and until I was sixteen I thought I was jinxed.

I avoided ladders, broken mirrors and was petrified of black cats. For four years, I thought I was unlucky and that nothing good ever happened to me. The reality of the situation was I wasn't unlucky, no one was out to get me and God wasn't angry with me. It was a belief that had negative implications because the more I thought about it the more I saw negative forces around me.

This is the basis of the law of attraction. This is why negativity is hard to get rid of. If you spend the day, wallowing in self-pity and thinking negatively then the negative forces around you will be heightened. This is why negative people can see the worst possible situations; for example, a negative person can complain constantly about the rain, whereas a positive person will see the blessings in the rain. The law of attraction is all about perspective, but that perspective can either have positive or negative ramifications on our lives.

The law of attraction encourages you to have the freedom to take control of how your future is shaped by your thoughts. The law of attraction is more than just a theory, it is a tool you can use to change your life.

## Ways You Can use It To Change Your Life

Whatever you believe, whether it is God or the universe, you need to understand that if you want success you have to change your mindset. It's important that you start understanding everyone is given the same opportunities at birth. Race, religion, background, and circumstances may factor into it, but God has no favorites. If life has been cruel to you then what have you done to make it like that. Sure, certain things are hard for some people, but often it's in our wiring that makes it harder. Even if you are having a hard time getting a job promotion, you are probably undoing your own efforts with your thoughts.

## You attract your experiences with your thoughts

When I went to college, I wasn't sure what I was going to do. So, I did a degree I had absolutely no interest in. It bored me to death. I would sleep in class because that's how much I disliked doing it. The people around me loved it and I thought maybe there was something wrong with me. A few people said I would fail because of my disdain for the degree.

I could have agreed with that statement and changed degrees, but I wanted to pass it not because I wanted to use it after school. I believe in finishing a task no matter how frivolous or tedious it may be. I knew I was where God wanted me to be and I would find a solution eventually. To my surprise when I graduated, I achieved the grade I wanted.

In life, whatever you think about will happen. If you see yourself poor then you will be poor. If you see yourself as a bitter old person then that's what's going to happen. If you see yourself in a good light that's what will happen. The world has two forces at play, good and bad. If you think positively the good forces will over overpower the bad. Our minds are more powerful than you might believe them to be.

## What you think about, will likely happen

As I said before I used to be very superstitious. I used to think some people were just meant to be the top guns and I wasn't. I thought about failure often and what happened was I failed.

Because it happened, I thought of myself as a failure. I didn't realize it originated from my thoughts. The way I saw myself and nothing I did seemed right. I had a light bulb moment when I was in college. Something clicked into place for me. In high school, I was terrified of speaking in public; so terrified that the thought kept me up at night. I wanted to be good at it, to shed my fear of speaking to a crowd of people I didn't know. As much as I tried, I failed each time at it, but I tried again in college. This time it was different. I didn't see myself stammering and failing miserably, I saw victory. What happened, to my surprise, was it worked. I had conquered my fear of public speaking. I spoke to a crowd of people I didn't know, who didn't know me, but they enjoyed the speech.

I was still terrified, but what had changed was I knew I could do it and I conquered my fears.

## Success is for everyone

Too many people think that God smiles on a few people and everything works for those people. Success isn't in short supply. Your boss who wears suits that look like thousands of dollars wasn't born in that suit.

Let's take Ophrah Winfrey, the first-ever black talk show host. She came from a broken home, was abused as a kid and was told that she was ugly. She got pregnant at fourteen and lost the child.

Bill Gates was a broke college dropout who couldn't make any money and his first business failed. Albert Einstein couldn't speak until he was four years old. Imagine that the world's most intelligent man couldn't speak until he was four. Jim Carrey was homeless, he dropped out of school at fifteen to support his family. Bethany Hamilton who won first place in the Explorer Women's Division of the NSSA National Championships had her arm bitten off by a shark when she was only thirteen. Richard Branson has dyslexia so does Orlando Bloom. Stephen King's book was rejected 30 times. Charlize Theron witnessed her mother kill her father at fifteen.

There are so many more examples, but my point is that everyone who is successful had obstacles they had to face, whether it be unwanted pregnancy at a young age, poverty, homelessness, murder, rejection, abuse or living in deplorable circumstances.

Remember that God doesn't play favorites. Success is something that can be achieved by anyone as long as you believe that.

# Don't wallow in disappointment

Do you remember how you feel when you are disappointed or sad? By the end of the day, I can guarantee that you will feel worse. It's alright to be disappointed in something not happening or an event that went wrong, but when you wallow, you only feel worse. You will have a heightened level of serotonin that will give you an acute sense of all the problems in the world and it will be hard to get over it. Serotonin is the hormone responsible for when you feel sad or disappointed.

# Avoid TV shows that have negative connotations

We are what we watch, eat, read and listen to. It's a scary thought, but if you watched TV shows that were violent growing up chances are you will be a violent child. Images are programmed into our brains over and over again. Said images affect us more than reading. The same can be said for your music. Your music is what defines you and jarring music can affect you negatively. We don't understand how it's important to be careful when it comes to entertainment. Whatever you do, make sure that it's building on you and that includes the books you read, what you watch when you are relaxing, the magazines you invest in and the music.

# You are responsible for your actions

Whatever you do and put out there will come back to you. Whether it be a relationship that has turned sour or a disagreement with a colleague. This includes what you constantly think about, how you act around your family and friends. You are completely responsible for everything. It's easier to blame some outside force for you losing your job. And as millennials, we have had a harder time than any other generation due to the social media platforms that constantly make us re-evaluate our lives. This is a reason why so many young people are floating around, but even though that may be the case you have to understand your emotions and actions. Be in control.

## See life as you hope it should be and not as it is

If you want to change the world don't focus on how life is not, but rather on how it should be. If there's an injustice you feel should be corrected then hope that it will be. This will give you a boost of optimism that will change how you look at life. The world isn't written in black or white or even gray. There are problems, but with every generation there were problems and that didn't stop people like Rosa Parks, Joan of Arc, Mark Zuckerberg, Walt Disney, and Galileo.

Their contributions vary from innovation to standing up to what they believed was wrong. You have a chance to imagine how the world will be like and work on it until it is. That belief will make the world a better place, but if you see the problems as being fixed and then you won't see a difference.

# How To Use The Law Of Attraction by Using Visualization

If you want immense change you need to visualize the life you want to have. You need to quieten down your mind for about fifteen minutes; think of nothing but positive images. Pray and meditate. Focus on all the blessings in your life and think of how you would like your life to be in six months to five years. Don't let go of your objectives. That way you understand what the end goal is all about.

# Parkinson'sLaw

*"Your work is going to fill a large part of your life, and the only way to be truly satisfied is to do what you believe is good work. And the only way to do great work is to love what you do. If you haven't found it yet, keep looking. Don't settle. As with all matters of the heart, you'll know when you find it." - Steve Jobs*

Recently, I learned that productivity is not about how hard you work, but rather how smart you work.
Driving yourself crazy to follow through with a task and spending weeks on that task only makes it more complicated.

This method may have worked twenty years ago, but there are far too many distractions now. Tasks that could be done within a couple of months are now being achieved in a few weeks. This may seem that you are taking time to actually, make sure the project is more thorough, but there's no urgency so the project comes out being sub-par.

Parkinson's law has been around since 1957, it means that "work expands so as to fill the time available for its completion."

A British Historian called Cyril Parkinson first observed this trend during his time with the British Civil Service. He noticed that once bureaucracies expanded they became more inefficient. He applied this principle to other circumstances and he saw there was a decrease in productivity and value once anything expanded. Cyril also discovered that simple tasks became more complicated if the allotted time frame given to them was far too long, but they became much simpler when the length of time was shortened.

We all have used Parkinson's law even if we didn't notice we were using it. Tasks that were assigned to us in college and instead of taking three months to do it you did it in a week. You surprised yourself by the high grade you got for a paper that took you a week instead of what you normally get when you complete a task in more than a month.

Tim Ferris's "4-Hour WorkWeek" talks about how you can do more in less time. Though Parkinson's law is beneficial, it also comes with its minuses. People tend to only do their tasks or follow through with their projects when time is running out. This will only lessen the value of the task because of the rush of adrenaline in finishing the project. Parkinson's law only works the way it's supposed to if you remember to work smarter and not harder.

You may be scratching your head and thinking that's what you are probably doing. Even people who seem like they are the most productive are actually unproductive because they aren't following certain guidelines. We all grapple with this, the unproductive bug.

Many people thrive on the excitement of doing a task when time is running out. This could lead you down a rabbit hole that's hard to come out of. Though doing a task in less time is better than lengthening the time for it. The results may come out as you are stressing yourself out and in turn, you won't put your all into the task.

It's been drilled into our brains for so long that working harder and not smarter is the best way to get things done. Working harder drains you more and you become more inefficient. Parkinson's law can change your life in ways you never imagined and once you know how to work smarter, you will have more time to do things that you actually love.

## Break down your monolithic tasks into smaller tasks

Let's say you have this task or project that has a far-away date and is cumbersome and monolithic. That task can easily be broken down into smaller and bite-sized tasks.

Write down each task with the time frame it should be completed. Make sure you half that time and focus on completing each task in a shorter time frame then you had initially planned for. By doing this you are concentrating on this one task and you are putting your all into completing it.

## Know what you're done means

It's all well and good to be a perfectionist if you are aiming for some kind of award for perfection. You must strive to be exceptional and not perfect. When doing a task, ask yourself whether you put all you had in it and had done enough work for it to be exceptional. That way you put less stress on yourself and you value the time you put in it.

## Have clear boundaries

The problem with Parkinson's law is most people think that they need to multitask in order to do more things in less time. Multitasking is the worst of the worst and it won't give you the results you want.

Our parents may have spoken of a time when they could do so many things at the same time. Multitasking doesn't make you more productive than those around you and in fact, it will make you less. Your focus is all over the show and our brains are not like computers, they take time to get back to the previous task. You could have used that time your brain was building up momentum to finish the task at hand instead of doing three tasks at once.

So, set clear boundaries. Look at your tasks and finish one task after the other. By doing this you know your task better because of the consistent time you spent on it.

## Know what's next

Don't spend too much time doing one task, complete it and move onto the next task. Keep the momentum burning. By doing that you will finish your to-do list a lot more quicker and by going onto the next task you will never feel like you are slacking off.

## Challenge yourself

We generally work better when we have a tight deadline or a challenge ahead of us. This makes us find ways to complete the challenging task in a tight deadline. Adding safety nets won't help you at all, you have to look at yourself realistically and figure out how long it will take you to complete the task.

## Use incentives as a motivator

Don't be too hard on yourself. When you accomplish your goals or task in the allocated time then reward yourself. Give yourself a pat on the back, go to the movies or do whatever you had been planning to do before the tasks.

## Using Time Management Theories to get ahead

Parkinson's Law is the key needed for time management. Used accordingly it can skyrocket your productivity and make life more efficient. Time management is something a few of us understand because of the complicated intricacies associated with it. It takes a while to understand how to work around it, achieve all you want to before the day is gone and to be as productive as you can be.

There are 1440 minutes a day. When a number that big comes into our mind we instantly get the big picture. You have enough time. It's all a matter of our perspective.

Parkinson's law is not the only theory you can use to have a more productive life, but it is one of the most popular theories being used. It presents an opportunity to be like the top managers by understanding the difference between being effective and ineffective.

## The pickle jar effect

This is the last important time management theory you should know about. Along with the other time management theories; the Pareto principle (go to chapter two) and Parkinson's Law.

This principle is particularly important because it illustrates what not to do rather than what to do. At times, we spend way too much time on trivial tasks that we think are important. The Pickle Jar theory illustrates this with a pickle jar, the pickle jar and its contents represent everything about time management. It is represented by rocks, pebbles, sand, and water.

Rocks are the important things that need immediate action and once achieved they reap massive results. The pebbles produce an effect but are not as important as the rocks. The grains of sand are small trivial tasks that are easy to do, require very little time or effort and are of very little importance. These are text messages, checking your mail and chit-chatting. This produces very little benefit.

The water represents all the very insignificant trivial tasks that fill up your time and make you idle. The key to knowing how to use this principle is to identify what are your rocks and when you know that you can increase the number of rocks in your life. You will need to diminish the amount of sand in your jar. The best way you can do this is by using a technique called batching. This basically means combining small tasks together for example instead of checking your email four times in an hour, do it twice a day.

## Piecing it together

If you have a problem with time management then you need to identify which theory could help you. You might not have problems with spending too much time on small tasks, but you might identify more with working too hard or maybe you assign too much time to each task. Whatever it may be, remember time management is something that can't be avoided. If you want to change your life around, be more productive and achieve more then you need to focus on time management.

Once you do that, you will find out that your days are far more productive, you will feel as though you have accomplished more and this will generate massive results. It's important to look at your daily tasks and ask whether what you are doing is benefiting you in any way. If it isn't you have to decide to minimize the amount of time or if you should just cut it from your daily routine.

*Chapter   Ten*

# Pushing Back

*"Nothing in the world can take the place of Persistence.
Talent will not; nothing is more common than
unsuccessful men with talent. Genius will not; unrewarded genius is
almost a proverb. Education will not; the world is full of educated
derelicts. Persistence and determination alone are omnipotent. The
slogan "Press On" has solved and always will solve the problems of
the human race." -Calvin Coolidge*

In life, it's important you understand what you can take and what you can't. There are so many experiences that craft us to be who we are and it all starts with understanding what is pushing you back. And often we don't know we are doing this because it has become the accepted norm in our lives and we take it.

Pushing back will give you more force and energy to push the dominoes in your life that used to be extremely difficult. Do you have moments when you feel so lost and confused? Times when you think you're worthless and agree with what others say? Have you ever found yourself looking into the distance and having absolutely no idea what you are going to do with your life? We have all had the moments when we question our worth, purpose and wonder whether we can truly make a difference. Don't listen to those voices. The ones that make you question everything because when that happens it's an endless spiral of negative results that you don't need in your life.

## Steps To Take

## Find out what your dreams are

Too often we let people decide what we should do with our lives. We get accustomed to the safety zone, to us being in a loop and this becomes the new normal. If you think back to when you were fifteen you had these dreams that were either shunned or ridiculed. Whatever it was, you changed course and went down a different route. You might not have wanted to go down that route but you did.

Your dreams at fifteen are different from your dreams now. Even though your dreams are different, you still have these dreams within you that you would rather not discuss. You might be worried about what people think or how they will react to you having dreams that they might not understand. When you look back in twenty years' time what would you like to see?

The answer to that question will tell you what action you should take and what you shouldn't do.

## Break traditional ideas

I grew up in a country where certain rules are placed when it comes to careers, most kids grow up wanting to be lawyers or accountants. There's absolutely nothing wrong with wanting to be a lawyer or an accountant as long as that's what you want to do not what you think is normal. Martha wanted to be a doctor and at eight years old and I found her to be the bravest person I knew. She knew without a doubt she wanted to save lives. One of my best friends, grew up wanting to be a psychologist and it's what she wanted. Not what was the norm.

Breaking traditional ideas has been one of the main traits that separate those from being successful to those who are not. Mark Zuckerberg changed the way we saw interaction. Pete Cashmore changed the way we saw information on the internet by creating Mashable. The Wright brothers changed the way people saw flight. There are numerous examples of people breaking traditional ideas.

Living by other people's rules and standards won't get you anywhere, instead, it will cause you to drift between what you want and what others expect from you.

## Be unreasonable

Too often we are told to be reasonable. Being unreasonable is shunned upon, people look at you as though you have lost your mind. So how can being unreasonable be the missing key to pushing back. Simple, the unreasonable dream big and bold, they come up with ideas that many see as stupid or ridiculous. Let's take a look at Madam C.J Walker who was a slave, many saw her as being unreasonable.

How could a slave with no money create a hair product line and be the first person to start the cosmetics industry. From being unreasonable. Stephen J. Cannell struggled with dyslexia in school. Many people thought him as being irrational for wanting to be a writer, but he did it anyway and wrote 21 Jump Street and the A-team.

Jim Carrey was a janitor and many saw his dream as wanting to be an actor as unreasonable. Henry Ford failed twice and that resulted in bankruptcy. Who would think it that he would revolutionize the automobile industry?

Being unreasonable doesn't mean that you are being difficult. You know what you want to achieve and what is acceptable. People will see it as being unreasonable, no matter what you do in life, people will never see you the way you want them to see you. It's in their belief system, the way they look at life. So why not be unreasonable? Why not change the way people look at things and change someone's life as a result of that?

## Persistence

It's so easy to give up on your dreams when something doesn't work out. It's so much easier to change route even when you don't want to because maybe you feel it's in the cards. You throw down those ideas that you planned your life around and go with what everyone wants. You give up. The harder the challenges, the more it seems like the only solution is to throw down the ideas and sit around.

In general, as humans we don't like obstacles, we find them to be tedious and not worth our time. It's programmed into our minds now. And we never find out how close we were too massive results. If J.K Rowling gave up then we wouldn't have Harry Potter. You are not J.K Rowling, but that doesn't mean you can't achieve what she did. It starts with persistence in the face of innumerable odds. When people tell you that you can't, keep going. When doubt floods in and all you want to do are run away, keep going. Never tell yourself you can't do anything. Believe that you were put in the world to change it and therefore regard yourself as persistent. Remember if you aren't living your purpose then you are doing a disservice to yourself and God.

## Believe anything is possible

So, you want to do marathons but think you can't. You want a promotion or to change your career, but think it's either impossible or too late to do so. You want to open up a restaurant, but don't think you can achieve it. I'm going, to be honest with you, all those excuses above are irrelevant and you are lying to yourself. As a baby, you couldn't walk or talk, but you learned how to. As a little kid, you couldn't swim or ride a bike, but you learned how to do that.

I was one of those kids who gave up slowly and as a result of that, I never learned how to swim or ride a bike. I thought it was impossible for me to do that and that became my normal. Unbelief is hard to get rid of once it sets in and the unfortunate part is we lose the resilience and belief we had when we were kids.

Do I regret not learning how to swim or ride a bike? What I know is if I really wanted to do that now I could learn how to do it. I couldn't do public speaking because of stage fright, but I wasn't going to allow that to be my new normal and I learned how. I didn't focus on the unbelief I had as a kid, I focus now on belief. Believe in the possibility of the impossible coming to fruition and when you do that you will be surprised by the results.

## Take risks

Being cautious is a deathmatch, that may be an over-exaggeration, but when we are cautious we limit ourselves. We limit what we can do or achieve and that affects what we do next. You are limiting your potential, worth and opportunities. So why do people not take risks? It all comes down to fear. The fear of rejection, acceptance, and failure.

People are terrified of losing out or failing, so much that they rather not go all out. They feel that is safer. Just because you are playing safe doesn't mean that you will not get burned. There are so many ways you could burn your fingers from what you are doing. Those who rather go out in life with gloves and protective gear miss out on life. They miss out on what they could do and achieve. They will never know what they can achieve if all they think of is falling down. And in that way, they will forever live a life that's short of being exceptional.

## How Bad Do You Want It?

Your future depends on what you want it to be like. If you want to change your life then you must ask yourself how badly do you want it. Do you think about it constantly? Do you believe that is your purpose? No one can tell you what your purpose is, but you. No one can point you in the right direction except you. All these are guidelines, but it will fall on deaf ears unless you truly want a 360-degree change in your life. Your values, morals, and ethics must align with your desire to change your life. If you want to be successful, find ways where you can achieve that by keeping your values intact. That way you know you won't compromise for anyone or anything.

## Will it be easy

Anyone who believes that success is easy has not gone for something with all they have. They haven't pushed themselves to the extremes and overcame numerous obstacles along the way. They haven't questioned their sanity. Anything worth something is not going to be easy. It's going to take a lot of work and a lot of fights. You will need to constantly fight for what you want. To push what is acceptable and declare that this is worth it for you.

## Have discipline

Successful people are extremely disciplined. We all struggle with it at times, but some do more than others. They regard it as a trait reserved for a few people. That's how I used to see discipline. As this hard to reach the goal that was far away, but discipline is basically having self-control and doing what you are supposed to do.

If you want this year to be great, you have to have enough self-control to not watch too many television shows or movies. You must be disciplined enough to go to bed early for you to wake up earlier in the day. Discipline is what will get you to higher peaks but it all starts with knowing what you should do and what should be stopped.

I didn't have much discipline as a kid, I spent way too much time watching television and too little time studying. As a result, I failed a lot in primary school. I knew I had a problem with school so the next step was for me to work at it, but I didn't.

## Get out of your comfort zone

Being in your comfort zone is what is stopping you from achieving 10x results. It is what is pushing you back and you need to step out. When you do that you will find out that you will meet more people, these people might not be the ones who are normally in your circle, but they will help you.

Getting out of your comfort zone will give you opportunities you never thought to be possible. Your perspective will change and in a positive way. Staying in your comfort zone is a clutch that will only push you back and never forward. It may be comfortable and familiar territory, but you will always be two steps back. The best thing is to be uncomfortable because it is only there that you raise your standards (go back to Chapter 3).

## Constantly learn

Depending on how much you want to change your life then you will require massive amounts of learning. Whatever it may be, focus on the importance of learning. Go to seminars and if you can't afford that then be ready to save money on attending one. Another thing is you can use online learning platforms such as udemy.com. It has literally anything you would like to learn and the majority of their courses are free. Keep feeding your mind and that will create the desired results.

## Stop the excuses

In high school, I used to come up with excuses for everything and when I didn't want to do anything I came up with an excuse. One of my friends back then pointed it out and it clicked. She was right, I came up with way too many excuses. Far too many that I often was stuck in one place and didn't move.

It might seem like the normal thing to do but it isn't. All you are doing is stalling your life and potential. It is stopping you from being all you can and you won't get anywhere with that. One common excuse is I don't have time. Everyone has 1440 minutes in a day so you have all the time in the world. If you don't have time to read in the day, cross out any activities that take away your time without giving you something back.

Alternatively, you can always read thirty minutes a day, that may seem like little time, but you would be amazed by how much you cover. Another excuse people love to use is I don't have money, there have been successful people who were literally broke or homeless and they managed to build businesses and become millionaires. What about what if I fail or I can't possibly do that? Truth is everyone who is anyone has failed many times and they also asked themselves the same thing.

Know your worth and stop lying to yourself. You have to be honest with yourself and look at the real reason you don't what to do that. You will find by knowing the reason you can find ways to fix that problem.

## Stop Procrastinating

I have a problem with procrastination so what I do is when I think about doing something I do it then and there. I have found by doing that I tick off my tasks for the day and that makes me feel good.

When I procrastinate a lot, I am annoyed with myself and I start to question what I'm doing with my life. Procrastination is itself is a tool that stops you from doing something, but it can only stop you if you let it. Start living your life today.

## Stop complaining

It's so easy to complain about everything, from politicians to the bad economy or those in authority. The question here is not what the problem is, but what you are doing about the situation. Complaining is a natural defense mechanism. You might at the moment feel relieved, but that doesn't eliminate the problem. It's still there. Whether it's how your boss treats you, the low pay, your being in debt or unemployed. No amount of complaining will take that way, instead, it will make you despondent.

I used to complain about everything, it doesn't mean that I don't complain here and there, but I have to watch myself. Complaining about the situation always makes it look worse than it actually is. You are alive. That in itself is a blessing. Complaining isn't going to solve your problems. It isn't going to fill your bank account. Your boss won't promote you if you complain. Your lecturer won't be easier for you if you complain. There are always solutions out there to fixing your problems. What you need to do is be open to finding the solutions.

# Chapter Eleven

# GoalPost

*"The big secret in life is that there is no big secret. Whatever your goal, you can get there if you're willing to work." – Oprah Winfrey*

Goals are crucial to our lives. They help us understand the direction we should go on and what we should avoid,

but if we never think about our goals we can never achieve success.

Some of the material in this chapter will be theoretic like Law of Attraction and Parkinson's Law. The principles follow what many have devised as being the most efficient ways to achieve goals. There are a couple of arguments that have been made that those theories don't work as well as many have said. The choice is yours to decide which theories to use and which ones to disregard. Everyone is different and therefore what might work for some won't work for others.

# Goal-Setting Theory

Two researchers, Dr. Edwin Locke and Dr. Gary Latham spent years researching goals and how to achieve them. In 1968, Dr. Locke wrote an article called "Toward a Theory of Task Motivation and Incentives." In the article, he showed that clear and precise goals motivate employees. Later on, he developed the theory to highlight that working on goals improves overall performance and progress. A few years later after Locke published his article, Dr. Latham researched goal setting in the workplace and his results supported Dr. Locke's findings.

# Locke and Latham's Five Principle

In their research, they found that goals need to meet five principles in order to improve the chances of success. When this is achieved, you are able to follow through with your goals.

1. Clarity
2. Challenge
3. Commitment
4. Feedback
5. Task Complexity

### Clarity

Setting clear goals is the objective. In order for you to achieve what you desire you must set goals that are clear.

Goals that are vague don't get you to where you want to be and often they will not motivate you.

## Be clear and specific

If it helps, use SMART to help you to be more clear and specific in your goal setting. The first step is to have a clear vision in your mind of what you want to achieve. If you want to exercise more, don't simply write down exercise more, but state what form of exercise you will do and at what time. For example, five times a week you will run a mile in six minutes. Whatever it is make sure it as clear as possible.

## Break down the goals in steps

Having lofty goals that haven't been broken down is hard to achieve for anyone. It's way easier if those goals have been broken down into small steps that lead to that big goal. For example, you want to be healthy. The way to do that would be to exercise for five to ten minutes a day. Eat food that is healthier, eat more vegetables and fruits. Go to the gym twice a week. Drink more water. This can be far more extensive.

## Track progress

It's crucial for you to track your progress. There are various apps out there that will help you in tracking your progress. When you have accomplished an important step, reward yourself so that you keep going.

# Acknowledge your weaknesses

We all stumble and fall, but that doesn't mean we are likely to fail. It just means that we need to understand where the problem is or our weakness. Appreciate those weaknesses they will make you work harder to achieve your goals. Then find out where you went wrong and work to ensure that you will work on that.

# Be accountable

Accountability is very important. Ask a friend to help you remain accountable. When you know you did not keep your word, you are more likely to push yourself to achieve that goal. Try creating a commitment contract on stickK.

# Enjoy the ride

The journey will be a long one to the new year, but if you enjoy it then time will fly. You are most likely to achieve your goals if you enjoy it.

# Setting Challenging Goals

The more challenging the goal, the more motivated you are to achieve it. Make sure the goal isn't too challenging for you.

# How to set challenging goals

Develop self-discipline so you can keep pushing yourself to follow through with your goals.

Is the goal challenging enough to spark your interest? If it isn't, you will eventually get bored.

Do your research so that you are realistic about the milestones and challenges you may face.

Identify how you can reward yourself after you accomplish a goal. Each milestone you reach, pat yourself on the back or do a mini celebratory dance.

# Commitment

Stay committed to your goals, whatever they may be and how challenging they may appear. This is the best way to be effective. Your success depends on commitment. You can't sway from following through the goals.

# How to remain committed

Use visualization as a technique for you to stay committed to your goals. Imagine how your life will look like once you achieve your goals.

Create a treasure map and this will remind you to keep working hard. You could also create a personal statement that will speak highly of the end goal in mind.

# Feedback

One of the keys to success is feedback. It's important to listen to people's viewpoints on your progress. As painful as it may be, this will give you an idea of what you should keep working on and what errors need more focus. Besides listening to other people, you should also give yourself feedback. If you are not making progress, look deep within and find out why you are not.

Schedule time in the week to analyze your goals and find out which areas you are not making progress in.

Learn to ask for feedback from others.

Use apps to help direct you, track and measure your progress.

The best way to measure progress is by breaking big goals into smaller goals and seek feedback on each milestone.

## Task Complexity

Take account of complicated tasks. Make sure you don't get overwhelmed while working on the goals. Complicated tasks are beneficial because it makes us work and think harder. Just keep yourself in check while you do it.

# How to set complex and challenging goals

Give yourself plenty of time when dealing with complex goals. Set deadlines for when you want to achieve each goal. Give yourself enough pressure to fulfill those goals.

If you start to feel stressed then it is a clue that the goals you set might be too unrealistic. Reassess your goals and make them simpler.

Break large and complex goals into sub-goals. This will stop you from being overwhelmed and will motivate you into achieving the goals.

# Six Golden Rules to Goal Setting

These golden rules will point you in the right direction. The reason why some goals don't work is that they don't follow the six golden rules.

## Goals must motivate you

Goals must motivate you, they must convince you to follow through with them. They must keep you up at night and you must strive to want to achieve them. Write down your why for wanting to achieve this goal. Set goals that are a priority to you, you don't want to set too many goals that you won't be able to achieve.

The goal must align with what you want to have in the end. It must thrill you and if it doesn't you won't follow through. Think of the end in mind and the goals must all link up together. That way you aren't overwhelmed.

## Set SMART goals

You probably heard about SMART goals. The basic principles of goal setting following the guidelines of SMART.

## Set specific goals

Goals must be specific and as clear as possible. Vague and generalized goals will not help you at all. Let's say you want to write a book, but you are unsure of what kind of book it will be or how long and how many months you will complete the book. If you are not specific, chances are you won't achieve the goal. Especially if the end in mind is not clear.

## Set measurable goals

Goals must have deadlines. There has to be an amount and date assigned to each goal. How much weight do you want to lose? How much money do you want to save in a month? If you are unsure then you can't guarantee you will achieve your goal in a month or two months. Progress is determined by understanding the power of the amount and date.

## Set attainable goals

Don't overwhelm yourself by setting goals that can't be attained in the time frame you have set. If it is unattainable all you will do is demoralize yourself and you will give up altogether. Setting a goal for you to make $500,000 in a year is unattainable if you don't know how to make money. Set realistic and challenging goals that will give you the right balance.

## Set relevant goals

Goals must be relevant to what you want if your goal is to be a motivational speaker, but you are spending the majority of your time learning how to cook gourmet meals. Your goals are not aligned and you will need to reassess what you want in life.

## Set time-bound goals

Each goal must have a deadline so you know when you should celebrate your success. Goals without deadlines are hard to achieve because you are not focusing on the outcome of the goal.

## Set goals in writing

Writing down goals makes them more real and it sticks. Don't make the mistake of writing down your goals on the computer, the physical act of using a pen and paper is far more powerful than anything out there. Writing down the goals will make it impossible for you to forget the goals. A great tip is to have a to-do list under each goal. Another great tactic is to use the words "I will" and not "I am going to or I would like to."

## Make an action plan

Action plans are often missed, but you need to know the steps that follow each goal. When you accomplish one step you cross it out. This is a clear way to identify what progress you have made.

## Stick with it

Keep going on. No matter how challenging it may be, the end of the journey is far closer than you think but you need to stick with accomplishing the goal. If you want to have an extraordinary life then be committed to achieving that and you will.

## Use The 90 Day Goal Plan

Todd Herman uses the 90-day goal to achieve his goals. This is the most efficient way to achieve your goals. Think of your goals in 90-day increments and not in lengthy periods like a year or three years.

Peter Voogd states you can change your life in six months. He often points out in his book "6 Figures to 6 Months," that you must focus on achieving a set of goals in three months. Chandler Bolt says you can write a book in three months. Your motivation is heightened in three months because you are focusing on achieving those goals in that set period.

Three months may not seem like enough time to accomplish your goals, but it will keep you focused and you won't be demotivated too quickly. Short time frames are easier to manage and you will see results a lot quicker.

# Chapter Twelve

# Self-discipline and Passion are not mutually exclusive

*"Self-discipline begins with the mastery of your thoughts. If you don't control what you think, you can't control what you do. Simply, self-discipline enables you to do think first and act afterward." -Napoleon Hill*

Not many of us have self-disciple and many people believe that they are not creative. They fail to see the whole picture and that is that self-discipline, creativity, and passion have more in common. A person who is talented and doesn't have self-discipline will fail. A person who is self-disciplined and isn't creative won't think out of the box.

A creative person who isn't passionate about the project is likely not to put their all in it.

Many people don't think of themselves as being creative which is illogical because everyone has a certain degree of creativity. There are of course people who are naturally creative, who can paint masterpieces just from memory or listen to a song and know how to play it without looking at sheet music. These people are of course are talented. Even if you can't write sonnets or a haiku, it doesn't mean you are not creative.

This chapter is extremely important because with it you will be able to plan and work around that brilliant idea that's been bubbling in your mind for years. Whether you want to be more self-disciplined so you get things done or want to know how to build up an idea this chapter is ideal for you.

As a kid I wasn't disciplined, I saw it as a chore and not as an opportunity to grow. Many people look at self-discipline as a quality few can possibly possess and because of that they avoid trying it. Creativity is seen the same way, self-disciplined people see creativity as a quality only the extremely talented possess and they can't possibly learn to be more creative. Any skill can be learned, there are certain rules that apply to self-discipline and creativity. By the end of this chapter, you will have a better understanding of self-discipline.

## What is self-discipline?

Self-discipline is the ability to do an action despite your emotional state. In everything we need to have self-discipline in order for us to accomplish a goal. Whatever you want in life you need to realize that self-discipline is critical to achieving it. Whether it be losing weight, getting high grades, building a business and writing a book. All this needs self-discipline. Usually what deters people from following is a lack of self-discipline and procrastination.

Self-discipline is one of many personal development tools out there, it can solve countless problems and give you the strength needed to overcome many things.

## The Pillars of Self-Discipline

There are five pillars of self-discipline which are acceptance, willpower, hard work, industrious and persistence. When you take the first letter of each word you get the acronym "A Whip."

## Acceptance

One of the five pillars is acceptance. If you want a change in your life you first need to agree with the reality of the situation and acknowledge whatever you perceive around you. Many people fail to accept whatever is around them and live in a bubble where they never move forward.

If there are chronic difficulties in your life the root of the problem is a failure to accept reality as it is. I used to believe I didn't have low self-esteem and whenever someone pointed that out I would get furious. "Who do they think they are?". "They don't know me and therefore don't get to judge me." I was so wrapped in my own world that I didn't want to listen to anyone and because I refused to accept the problem. I kept failing and didn't realize what the problem was until everything I tried went belly up.

You can't solve the problem if you don't know what the problem is. You don't know how strong you are until your strength is tested. You can't move forward if something is pulling you back.

If you want to increase your self-discipline then you need to know where you stand right now at this moment. The below questions will help you out, write down ten questions to add to this list and answer honestly. No one knows you more than you. If you can't accept your situation then you are either being ignorant or you are in denial.

Either way, you are working on developing yourself, your perception is fuzzy and you have a false reality. If you can't accept that you are not fit and think you can bench press then you are in denial. The first step to success is accepting reality and developing a training regimen around it. So, step up your game and figure out what you can and can't do. Only then can you move forward.

## Here are a few questions to ask yourself:

How much time do you waste on a typical day?

What are you doing to change your life?

Do you have any addictions? Caffeine, nicotine, sugar, etc

Could you fast for one day?

How much-focused work could you do in a day?

If you lost your job do you have an idea what you would do if you couldn't get another job?

Can you give up something you love for thirty days?

How would you rate your self-discipline on a scale of 1-10

## Willpower

Willpower is the ability to control your emotions, thoughts, and actions in order to achieve what you want. Willpower like self-disciple is a mental muscle and you need to consistently exercise the muscle. People who are happier and more successful have a lot of willpower. Willpower is that secret sauce we all need to change our lives, that stop us from continually messing up our lives and fashion habits that will help us out.

The unfortunate part is willpower is a mental muscle that appears limited, it drains us both emotionally and physically. Most times the easier choice is not to fight something and because of that willpower is underutilized. There are of course many ways you could increase your willpower including eating the right meals, take one change at a time, get a good night's sleep, steer clear of temptation and develop small but powerful habits. This isn't an exhaustive list of ways to increase willpower.

Remember because willpower is a mental muscle you require enough energy in order to increase it. By finding ways to increase it you will have an abundance of willpower and this will develop your self-discipline. By focusing on one pillar you will cause a chain reaction and the other pillars will be easier to adapt to your routine.

## Hard work

Hard work will challenge you, it will compel you to go the extra mile and it will be exhausting both mentally and physically. Because of the challenge, you will constantly have to find ways to adapt and problems to solve. Many people try looking for the easiest path and because of that their lives are not all they could be.

Hard work comes with strong results. You could get lucky and get to there without hard work, but can you repeat the process. Everything in life comes with sacrifice and knowing what you want out of life. If you want to be successful then you need to know that the one way to get there is through hard work. Get rich quick schemes don't work. Neither do all the fast and easy schemes people promise online these days.

Successful people or those who live extraordinary lives all have to deal with hard work. They have to consistently push the limits and discover what's exceptionable and what's not. They have to be on the go. Hard work goes hand-in-hand with acceptance. We all have to come to accept the things in our lives that require our attention. Hard work doesn't mean over exhausting yourself, you basically have to put effort into what you want to get.

## Industry

Being industrious simply means putting in the time to get what you want whether it be challenging or easy. You have to put in the time. This is one of the most important factors of self-discipline. It takes a lot of self-discipline to sit down or to put in the time when it is needed. Many problems are amassed because people refuse to put in the time, they don't work on what's needed and the problem becomes worse. Ignoring something doesn't mean it will disappear like the saying goes "out of mind and out of sight."

Just because you don't think about it and do anything about it doesn't mean it will go away. How many problems are on the to-do list that you have been ignoring? When you are industrious you will find that your day will be more productive then it was before.

## Persistence

Persistence is the ability to continue pressing on or going after something regardless of your emotions. It is easy to give up, to throw in the towel and walk away. Few people persist and that's why many people live mediocre lives.

There were many times that I wanted to give up, to be what many people thought I would become. If I hadn't I wouldn't be writing this book, I wouldn't have gone to university or graduated. Motivation will only get you so far, what will get you to the end is persistence. Knowing that giving up won't give you the desired results. You will get results if you persist, it may not appear as though you are getting results, but everything takes time and so does success.

One of my friends wanted to become an accountant. Though she kept failing the exams for her to be accepted in a prestigious accounting firm she kept pushing. That is determination. She had to redo the year twice, many would have chosen a different path, but she knew what she wanted and went after it. Persistence sometimes isn't the right path for you, but that is for you to decide. If you are studying law, but your passion is in Art then persistence is the wrong move. Figure out where you want to go and consistently work at that.

Importance of Building Self-Discipline

If you want to make headway you need the self-discipline to do that. You need to constantly train so that you strengthen your self-discipline if you don't the weaker you will become. Do progressive training, when you accomplish one challenge then go for the next and next. Continually be moving, that way you are strengthening your self-discipline. Don't keep working on the same challenge. That won't help you at all, it will keep you on the same level as you were before.

Don't make the mistake of pushing yourself too far. This will take time, don't try to change your life overnight, you will fizzle out. Instead, remember baby steps are far more rewarding than leaping over hurdles and hurting yourself.

If you are undisciplined then work on  A  Whip. Research ways to be more disciplined. Procrastinate less.

Accept that you need to change your life, persist even if the odds are against you, work smart and be industrious.

## Passion versus Self-Discipline

## Passion + Action = Results

Remember the above equation as the ultimate formula for success. Passion by itself won't get you to the top, you maybe passionate about cooking, but if you are not acting on it then it's pointless. If you heard that talent only gets you so far. This is so true. Most talented people work less than those who are not because they feel they don't have anything to prove.

Due to that those who are less talented often get to the top. This depends also on the person and what they see as being important to them. Passion is not required for success, self-discipline and action are, but passion makes the journey far more enjoyable. Passion will wane like most fuels.

I won't recommend using passion as the only fuel for success. In whatever you do remember what you need is to understand what will get you the results you desire. Action will get you the results so will self-discipline and passion is the motivator at times needed.

# Chapter Thirteen

# Creativity and Risk-Taking are the Key Ingredients

*"Every child is an artist, the problem is staying an artist when you grow up." Pablo Picasso*

As a kid, I used to dream about my life. The way I wanted it to be and I ignored all that was around me.
There were things I did differently than others, for one I couldn't color within the lines and that was not acceptable. I have always been the creative type, probably because of my disdain for following the rules.

Everyone is born creative, as kids, we come up with these fascinating ideas that are shunned. The world values our creativity only when it suits them, but when we color outside the lines then that makes us different. No one likes to stand out against the crowd. We don't like to see the disapproval in their eyes as we tell them about our plans or ideas. Many of us spend our whole lives trying to fit in and we might not even know this. To fit in we have to break away from our creative selves and be a molded person.

Successful people in any industry are different because they didn't allow people to mold them to the versions they want them to be. They went their own ways and discovered how to do something better. Creativity is the greatest quality you will ever have, never overlook its importance in your life and how far you will go with it.

## The Perception of Creativity

There are two main schools of thought when it comes to creativity. Some people believe it to be a burden, egregious and a skill that won't get you far in life. These people tend to be those who haven't focused on their creativity, the world has burned them and they have lost hope. These people tend to be those who had big dreams, but because of how the world perceived them they chose to walk on a path everyone walks on. They live a life full of regret and always ask themselves the question of what if.

The other school of thought which many successful people believe in is that creativity gives you a burst of energy, that big dream that can change the world and will help you think out of the box.

Society wants us not to be creative because if we are then we will want to go out on our own. Everyone is different. Many enjoy working for other people. It's not a bad thing to do that, but maybe you don't want to run your own business. It could be you want to be a writer, chef, blogger, podcaster or have your own talk show.

Whatever it may be, creativity helps you craft the decisions for you. Studies show that many people before they turn 30 are miserable because they go to jobs they dislike. Their employers shun their big ideas and they are stuck behind a desk looking through the window at those below. Some stare at their computer screens for hours waiting for time to run out. Many go through their classes wishing they had chosen differently.

They stay within the lines of what is possible and come up with excuses for why not to do anything. People often complain too much about a situation, here are a few examples.

I'm African, Asian, white, black, short and etc

I don't have money

I can't write

I am not good enough

I need a job with a steady income before I choose to

follow my dreams

My parents won't approve

What will my friends think?

I'm too young, I can't possibly start a business

It's too late

The economy is bad

The country I live in is not the best environment

I'm a mother or father

Our reasons or excuses shouldn't stop us from going out and achieving our dreams. Creativity will find a solution or idea that can help you in any situation. We are brainwashed to the point that all we see are problems. No problem can stop you from achieving what you want except you. People are coming up with so many concepts and ideas, what separates them from you? The simple fact is they allowed their creativity to take them to places you are too scared for it to take you.

The world will say creativity won't pay the bills, but what you produce will generate results and pay the bills. Can everyone be creative? Yes. Some are just too afraid, but when you allow creativity to change the way you think your life will change.

## Where Does Taking Risks Come In?

Creative people take more risks than most people. If Steve Jobs didn't push the Mac or the Ipad forward, where would we be? It was the biggest risk for him to do that, his team said it wouldn't work, but Steve Jobs had an idea and knew it would work. A movie like La La Land shouldn't have won so many awards like it did because the premise around it has been done for so many decades, but Damien Chazelle had a vision for the movie. J.K Rowling took a risk in accepting that Harry Potter be adapted into a movie.

Risks are what create innovations, they are what change the world and not every risk turns into success. Failure is part of the process. The point is not in failing, but in the lessons, you learn from the failure.

## Why people don't like taking risks?

People are terrified of taking risks, it freaks them out because they don't want to fail. If you want to be successful then failure and rejection are guaranteed. You have already failed by default if you are not doing anything with the ideas you have. It may not seem like it, but the fear of failure has stopped you from making a difference.

Fear is fake events appearing real. Keep that constantly in your mind. Einstein took risks, he couldn't swim and yet he loved sailing. A man who loved being in the water, but couldn't swim and that didn't stop him.

Risk-averse people despise the unknown and that's what taking risks means. You will never know whether it will lead you to success or a dud. Not every idea is a stellar grand plan, not every idea will change the world and there are ideas that are really terrible.

You may fail, but that process of failing will teach you something in the future. People who play it too safe remain in the same position there are in today, ten years later. They rather stay in their comfort zone, but they will never achieve what they want to achieve in life. You may be too terrified to do something many may regard as ludicrous. You are not alone if you are going through this.

# Here are a few ways you can overcome the fear of taking risks;

## Focus on the positives and not the fear

If you let fear control you then you will never do anything. Focus on the positive outcomes of the situation and not on the negatives. When you do this, you will see the brighter side and that will push you into taking risks.

## Just do it

We talk ourselves out of doing things and that's the problem. Just do it. Think of what might happen if you don't and then go for it. Have the courage to pursue your dreams no matter how preposterous they may seem. Give yourself props, you are a sane person and this dream is a manifestation of what you want in life. Stop the excuses for doing something, they aren't responsible for why you didn't do something with your life. It's you.

## Keep fueling your creative juices

Keep working on becoming more creative, by doing this you are making it possible for you to take risks. Give yourself time and focus on what you need out of life. Then work on that idea, think of how that idea will help the world and your family. Ignore everyone who has nothing positive to say and you will discover you will become braver.

# Dare to Dream

Dare to think bigger, to explore unknown territories and to be different. We all have dreams and to get there you need to be willing to put it all on the line. To show the world that this is me. We all have a purpose; this ability to see things differently from each other, but fear holds us back.

Many people choose not to risk anything and they never live a boundless life. Then there are those who don't take calculated risks. They jump with two feet and often land flat on their backs. I encourage you to take more risks, to focus on the creativity within you and change your life. However, whatever you want to do, it will take a lot of work. Take calculated risks. Creative thinking isn't easy.

Authors spend months on one novel, singer-songwriters spend hours holed up in studios writing a few songs and dancers have to figure out new dance routines often. Coming up with ideas is not easy and neither is executing those ideas. You are taking a risk working on your dreams. Often people are too scared to attempt that, why quit a job that pays them just enough to work on something that might take time to happen.

There's a quote I love it talks about how if you don't build your dreams then someone will hire you to build theirs. You will spend so much of your time building a dream that's not yours. Why not spend that time building your dream? Why not take the risk? Marie Forleo had a dream and at twenty-three she pursued it. She knew she wanted to motivate people and build a business empire.

What it took were guts, risk, and creativity. She had to work menial jobs so she could get enough money for her to do that. Everyone takes risks differently, but their risks payout. Take the risk to spread the word about what you are doing. Take the risk to venture out and turn your dream into a reality.

# Chapter Fourteen

# The Three Other Key Ingredients

*"The difference between success and failure isn't the absence of fear but the determination to pursue your heart's desires no matter how scared you are." -Martha Beck*

When I was a little kid I wasn't sure who I was and therefore I was terrified of failure. I believed strongly that by figuring out who I was, I would fail and the thought made me not want to figure it out. The older I got the more I realized that courageous people still have fears, those who figure out who they are and what they want still fear the future.

What I have realized is a success is more than just figures and how much money is in your wallet or in the bank. It is primarily about reaching your potential, using your influence to inspire and change the world and helping people in need. It is about making sure those around you are comfortable. Success is your responsibility, duty, and obligation.

As I have said in previous chapters it won't be easy, but then again nothing is easy in life. We all have this assumption that reaching the top is far too hard and we aren't capable of doing that which is the wrong perception. Success is all about knowing the rules and following them. Understanding the key factors or ingredients in accomplishing greatness is a crucial step. Creativity and taking risks are two of the most important key factors to get to the top. Without it, you have no idea about building or developing something and without creativity, you will never take risks.

The other three ingredients in this book are also critical to achieving success in your life. We all have untapped greatness and potential. This part of us that screams for more, but few of us will go there due to the nagging voices in our minds.

Congratulations on coming this far. Studies show the majority of people will buy a book, read it to some point and never finish it. Anyone who has ever been cash-strapped understands how dispiriting it feels and how it is easy to get swept up in the frenzy of constantly wanting to do more, but never getting the chance to do that.

## Determination

Determination encompasses a lot of things such as being unreasonable, being interested in results, committed, courageous and persistent. To be successful you need heaps of determination and to continually persist in your pursuit of success.

Persevering regardless of the outcomes around you, your perspective changes, it puts a fire in you that can't be quenched and you keep getting up no matter what.

Being determined is one of those valuable tools we often overlook. When you are determined the words "no", "not possible", "I can't do this" or "not enough time" don't stay in your mind. That's extremely important.

We all need the drive to succeed in our dreams and visions because there will be a time when few will believe in your dreams and you will have to fight to be heard over the crowd. Determination will be the force that will push you when nothing else seems to push you.

As millennials, people have different perceptions of us, we are misunderstood because what drives us isn't money, but passion and wanting to change the world. Caleb Maddix wrote "Keys to Success For Kids" at twelve years old because he wanted kids to be able to make their own success stories. Nathan Chan created Foundr so he could inspire young entrepreneurs to change their lives. Joel Brown started addicted2success.com because he wanted to create a place to inspire young people and motivate them to change their outcomes.

Jared Kleinert wrote "2 Billion Under 20" with Stacy Ferreira to inspire people under twenty to take control of their dreams by sharing stories of millennials who were doing exactly that. A few years later he wrote "3 Billion Under 30" to showcase another group of millennials around the world following their dreams despite the odds.

They were all determined to do more than most people and though the odds seemed against them they kept going. Age, race, background and the economy can't stop you from achieving what you want. If you don't have a drive, then you can't move from where you are. An object in motion will remain in motion unless a force pushes it out of motion.

Our determination comes from various things, mine has come from constantly being told when I was younger I wouldn't amount to anything. It was drummed into me, I wasn't good at sports, academics or even art. It took me a while to find my way, but that's the thing everyone is different, but what unites us is wanting to make a difference. Determination comes in after our passion has been molded and once we have that nothing can stop us.

## No one can stop you but you

Often it's easy to talk ourselves out of something by giving excuses. Determination curbs that because when you want something bad enough then everything else doesn't seem all that important. It all depends on what you want in life and if you are willing to work to get it. Waking up at 4 am isn't easy, many successful people suggest waking up at

5 am, but when you want to go the 10x mile then you have to be different. Seeing yourself as a brand isn't easy.

Walking up the ladder and holding on even when the odds are against you isn't easy. Nothing is easy, but when you are determined then you keep going at it. What do you want your reality to be like? What do you want your life to be like? Times are changing, jobs are not as easy to get as they were and if you are employed, there's no guarantee you will have it ten years down the line.

Besides that, we don't know how much time is on our clock and every day we are hit with that realization. At eight-years-old, I almost died. I ran through a sliding door, the glass shattered and pierced my legs. The wounds were so bad that I could have bled to death if I hadn't gone to the doctor in time. I started to wonder what my purpose was and found out that death as much as we want to ignore it is out there. As I am writing this, a guy I knew from high school died because of a blood clot in his leg and that moved to his heart.

Look around, this is your life. Your legacy depends on what you want out of life, one day you will look back and wonder what you did in your twenties and early thirties. Scott Dinsmore when he was in his twenties created Live Your Legend and when he was climbing Mount Kilimanjaro he was hit by falling rocks. He left behind a legacy for his family and people will remember him for changing the world. Scott was only thirty-two. Though many told Scott his vision wouldn't work, he knew otherwise and went for it. People ignored him and didn't bother listening to him, but he proved that when you believe anything is possible you can move mountains. People will tell you that you are being ridiculous, foolish or naive to think you can make a difference. As long as you believe them then they are right.

## Just Do It

What are you waiting for? Time, money, a better economy, less pressure at school or work, an opportunity or you are not sure. Procrastination affects our lives in many ways and often we don't notice it. Many people come up with excuses or reasons for not doing something.

Successful people don't sit around, fiddling their fingers and waiting for an opportunity. For so long, I stopped myself by saying nothing was right and I couldn't start. It was a foolish notion because Isaac Newton waited for no one. Neither did H.G Wells, Thomas Edison, Ophrah, Richard Branson, and Steve Jobs. They didn't wait for opportunity, they saw what surrounded them and worked around that.

Everything falls into place when you start doing something, if you have no idea how to start a blog, just do it. Everything will become clearer once you just do it. If you are unsure how to start a business, write up an idea, or research business ideas and start from there. Look at your community and see the problems your community is dealing with. If you don't have money start with as little as you can, it's $3 to $10 for web hosting, getting your presence out there is the starting point.

Don't wait around for anyone to open the doors for you they won't. Millennials have far more opportunities to change the world than any other generation, we can start a business with little money. What it takes is starting and everything will come together.

Take action and your perspective will change, you will find yourself consciously making an effort to develop your idea.

## Circle of Influence

The people around you are very important, studies say you are the average of the five people you spend most of your time with. Your circle of influence includes those who are playing the game at a higher level than yourself and those who support you. Some people have a supportive group of friends first then the rest follows.

## Importance of community

We all need a community to rally us because though the road to success can be solitary it doesn't have to be. It can be hard to face obstacles alone and it is important having people support you and encourage you. There will be days when you want to give up, days when you want to lie in bed and do nothing.

I wouldn't be here if it wasn't for the people who supported me. I would have given up writing if I hadn't called my friend and told her. She was residing in South Africa at that time, Ruva told me that would it be a stupid decision to do and constantly reminded me never to give up.

I would have given up if Martha wasn't one of the first people to make me see my worth in primary school. I have so many people in my life who believed in me more than I believed in myself. My family is my rock and in times of doubt gives me encouraging words so I keep going at it. I could go on and on about the amazing people who encouraged me through my life, but that's not the point. They are a part of my story.

Just like you have people who support you and help you in your life. They are part of you and your story. Be it an Aunt Matilda who always knows the right thing to say to you, or your father who constantly reminds you that you can achieve the impossible or your childhood friend who never bashes your ideas, but encourages you. Know that you are never alone on this journey, you have to keep going at it. No matter what.

## Remove toxic people

Just like they are people who will believe in you, most people won't. It's part of life, going out there alone you will know who is in your corner and who isn't. There will be people who are quick to point out your faults and who always seem to say something negative. In whatever stage you are at, these people exist to push you forward. They are the hurdles you must jump over and the negative comments you have to ignore.

They went through a period when they were told they wouldn't amount to anything and believed in the words. They got hurt, fell down and didn't get up. When they see you going for it, they feel regret and the hurt all over again and that causes them to lash out.

My suggestion is only to keep people who value you, lift you up and encourage you. Relationships are about giving value and not just taking. Be careful who you let into your life, bad habits are easy to pick up on and you don't want to stop believing in yourself because of the toxicity of the people around you.

## Have a mentor

We all need mentors, whether it be books that you are invested in or a physical mentor. A mentor will keep pushing you. They have been where you are and know how difficult it is. Finding a mentor is easier than you think it is, it's all to do with how willing you are to push yourself out there.

A mentor will make the journey a lot easier for you, they will develop your idea into something clearer and will support you more than anything. They want what's best for you and because of that, they will keep helping you. Every successful person has at least three or more mentors, it might be hard to believe, but even Tony Robbins has a mentor. Grant Cardone has a mentor. Mentors are there to give you ideas on how you can apply a 10x attitude and tackle your problems head-on.

## Networking

Networking is extremely important, through it you are reaching out to people who could get out your message in the best way possible. By doing this you form a relationship that is fortified and will help you grow. People forget how important it is to network, they feel like they will be rejected if they go out there and rather stay in their comfort zone.

If you do that you will never make it. Simple fact. You must believe in your dream more than anyone and be willing to tell people about it, some will reject your idea, but many will be invested in your dream. The truth about success is those who are successful admire anyone who is going after their dreams. They are not jealous or even uninterested, to successful people, one success story is a success story for everyone.

# Other Key Ingredients

## Attitude determines altitude

Your attitude towards life says a lot about you. When you see a problem and the way you approach it is negative you won't go far. It is crucial that you have the right attitude and mind frame. If you are positive then even if things go awry you won't lose hope. Whatever you believe, you will conceive. Whatever you focus on will come to fruition.

## Seek to solve problems

There will always be problems, ignoring them won't cause them to explode. If there is a problem, seek out a solution. Not all problems will be easy to solve, but when you focus on solving one problem than solving the others will be a lot easier. When you solve problems, you will find that everything will fall into place.

## Have big goals and dreams

Never limit your potential or greatness. Never underestimate your value or worth and what you can bring to the table. Have big goals, when you have small goals it's easy to miss the mark than when you have big goals. You don't want to limit what you can do when you live in the generation of opportunity. Sure this time has more problems but set yourself apart from the rest by making a difference. Have big dreams that leave a footprint, that impacts a generation and changes the world.

## Be Courageous

Fear will tell you that you can't make it. People will say that you aren't that important. Lewis Howes suffered from dyslexia as a kid, he passed through life not thinking he was good enough. He went to university to play pro football when his father had an accident during his time in college. Lewis was on his own, his father couldn't pay for his fees anymore. To make matters worse, Lewis got injured while he was playing and couldn't play football anymore.

The one thing that had set him apart was gone. He sat on his sister's couch for years until he had enough and chose to help people with LinkedIn. With time, he became known as an influencer and traveled around the States doing seminars. He was only twenty-three at the time and it should have terrified him, but didn't stop him from continually growing.

He also set up a successful podcaster called "The School of Greatness" and has interviewed the most successful people on the planet. Over the years his podcast has become one of the best.

Lewis could have allowed his disability or misfortune to stop him. But he didn't, he ventured into the unknown and started traveling and speaking at events. Years later Lewis Howes is a bestselling author, his story has inspired thousands of people to find their passion and go for it.

Don't let fear stop you from pursuing your dreams, being courageous doesn't mean that you are fearless. Being courageous is about stepping out there despite your fear.

## Go looking for an opportunity

When one door opens another door closes. Successful people don't wait for opportunity, they go looking for it. Whether it be writing a book and self-publishing it. This provides the opportunity for people to know your name and become an authority figure. Whatever it is don't wait for an opportunity to come to you, instead keep going for it and you will certainly find it.

## Remember where you came from

It's important to remain true to who you are, whatever is thrown your way, it will not deter you. When you get to the top or achieve massive results it can be overwhelming if you forget who you are. Many people lose sight of where they came from and what they stand for.

If you don't know what you are fighting for, you get caught up in nefarious activities that you shouldn't get involved with. Stay true to who you are, put your foot down and keep fighting for what you believe in.

Be Humble, ethical and sincere

Don't forget where you came from, that is extremely important. Your background is the reason why you are the person you are today. The people in your past helped shape you, whether it was believing you or helping you along the journey. They played an important role in your life.

Never boast about your success and what you achieved. Be ethical in everything you do and be sincere. More opportunities will come to you if you understand how important it is to have a personality many will envy. Sincerity is one of the most valuable personality traits, people want to deal with those who are humble, sincere and ethical.

# Chapter Fifteen

# Your Story

*"What we do for ourselves dies with us. What we do for others and the world remains and is immortal" -Albert Pine*

We all have a story to be told, something that will be written about us or a tale people will tell when we are gone. Death may appear ominous because of many of we fail to realize there's no reset button to live. You can't go to sleep one day, wake up the next day and go back in time.

When one day is gone, you can't go back and make things right. Twenty-four hours is enough time to do a lot, but when you don't plan what you want to do with your month the days fly by too quickly. Have you ever had one of those months when you can't remember what you achieved or what you did? When you look back at your past year, what are the achievements that made your year? Does it make you blissful, satisfied or do you ponder what you are doing with your life?

Not everyone dreams about having a fortune five hundred company, being an entrepreneur or blogger. Some people just want to make a difference, whether it be running an NGO or creating a show for young people to go to. Other people want to be missionaries, spread love and heal the world. Others dream of being pilots, but they changed route because they thought they wouldn't make it.

Whatever your dream is it's your dream. Your vision and if you believe in it then nothing can possibly stop you. Will it take time? Everything in life will take time. We all need a foundation to rely on and you might have no idea how to go to the next part of your journey. We all don't know how to get there, but we do know we would love to. There are dozens of free resources out there to fuel your passions, to inspire you and guide you on your journey. The start begins with now.

## What to take into consideration

Fourteen chapters are not enough to demonstrate all the ways you can change your life. However, these steps have been tried and tested. The short examples of people in this book I had come across when I was figuring out what was next. I got inspired by their stories. Their bravery in the face of adversity and they all had one thing in common, they didn't know how to start, but they did.

Starting is the easy part. It is asking yourself what you want in life, do you want more disposable income? Do you want to travel? Do you want to be a stage actor or sing in a band? Do you want to spend more time with your family? Do you want to love what you do? Live a life that's extraordinary.

Success changes from person to person. Some people want to be able to travel without thinking about whether they can afford it. One of my childhood friends is able to fly all over the world, he constantly is improving on himself and though many saw him as the joker in school, he has made a name for himself.

## We are own worst enemies

Do you feel the urge to do more, to be more, but think you can't? We spend our lives allowing people to dictate who we are and where we should go. The road can be a tireless place to walk and we carry heavy loads on that journey. We all have a purpose and not following it is doing a disservice to God, yourself, your family and your community.

Words have no claim on us until we let them. And we are all a slave to words unless we understand the power they have over us and stop listening to the negative words that pull you back. In high school, I knew a kid who everyone thought was crazy, his parents and the teachers saw him as a problem because he thought differently from everyone. There were moments when he would say the most profound things, but everyone saw him as a nutcase. When the world has rid you off and you listen to their words it's not the world's fault for what you do with your life.

As millennials, we live in a world constantly changing when people as young as twelve are millionaires and writing bestsellers. Excuses come and go, but the root of the excuse is still the same. Fear will stop and control you from pursuing your goals, but fear has built a seed in you because you allowed it. You allowed people to say that you were not good enough, you allowed them to steal your dream and stop you from going all out.

## Actions speak louder than words

It's hard to get motivated. There will be days when all you want to do is lie in bed and listen to sad songs. The key to anything in life is understanding that actions speak louder than words. Blowing your trumpet isn't going to bring momentum into your life if you are not doing anything. Telling people that you are doing A, B and C won't make it true if all you are doing is saying it.

If you want to be motivated then get to work. Momentum comes when you are continuously working on your goals. Often people talk about wanting to do something and they procrastinate. The problem with procrastination is it will always convince you that there's always tomorrow when tomorrow comes, you continue on this downward spiral of postponing what you are meant to do.

If you want to do something then do it then, procrastinating will only stop you from leading the life you want to have. It will continue to control what you do and when you do it. Lead by spending your time working on what you want.

## Misconceptions about Success

## You need to be perfect to be successful

Success doesn't need you to be perfect because we will never be. Being successful isn't an esoteric god-like quality where you need to always be sharp and on your game. Success is about going after your dreams and ambitions, it's about having the right mindset and not letting doubt cloud your mind.

## You need to have everything sorted at first

Going after your dreams doesn't mean you have to have everything sorted. The best way to reach your potential is by going after things that terrify you. We all have this potential within us but we are far too terrified to do anything with it. Joel Brown didn't know how to be a motivational blogger before he built Addicted to Success. What about Pete Cashmore who created Mashable? Did he understand how to create a site that would connect the masses through sharing information? Nathan Chan had no idea how he would contact influencers to interview for his magazine, but he still did it.

Not everything will be clear, all you might have is one idea, but that idea is enough motivation to push you to pursue your dreams. If you have an idea and think everything is going to land on your laps then you are mistaken. The years will pass and that manuscript will still be unpublished, you will still be working in a job you immensely despise. and hoping that you finally enjoy what you do. Not taking action is the worst thing you can do for yourself and letting go of your dreams won't make you any happier.

## Success is all about money

Success is about building a better world for future generations, it's living the life you want and doing what you love. It's not a solitary profession or one that discounts other people. If you were to look at every successful person, the majority of them are involved with changing the world, creating organizations that help people in the developing world or helping people find their calling.

Being successful is about being unreasonable in your pursuits and with time successful millennials have changed what success represents.

Ted Nash started his first online company at twelve years old. At the time, he was too young for him to take full control of the company. He spent the next couple of years raising funds from angel investors and created his first app that was downloaded one million times. Ted became the first teenager to achieve that.

Success is different for anyone, for Ted it wasn't about the money, he wanted to build something for his family and friends. Even when he created Tapdaq, it was about giving app developers a way for them to promote their apps.

## You can be successful all by yourself

Success is a community, it's about helping each other up and lending a hand. Often people think that they can get to the top without helping other people up. That is the wrong mindset, successful people all help each other. They advertise the other person's projects to their community, they are willing to go out and help someone. Being successful isn't about thinking of yourself and your goals. It isn't about wandering the road alone and thinking you don't need anyone's help.

What value can you give to them whether it is advice or helping them execute their plan? Success is about networking and building.

## Seeing success as a goal

Success comes as a reward of doing something just like money. You can't say you want to earn $1 million dollars in a year, but how are you doing that? No one is going to give you a million dollars. Success is the same thing. We all want to be successful, but we are not doing what successful people do. We spend most of our days just passing time and you think that will make you successful.

Success is the end goal, but you have to work at it to get it. Continually moving will get you there. But you need to work at it and create something that will change people's lives.

# My problems will disappear once I'm successful

Why do most people who win the lottery become broke within a year? Why do many people who become rich are still dysfunctional? The answer to that is simple, they put too much value on money and think it will make their problems disappear. If you are greedy, money is only going to heighten that quality. Many people say money is the root of all evil, but that saying has lost it's meaning along the way. Money doesn't change people, it only heightens their qualities.

Far too many people see money as the problem solver. Money can change your circumstances, but no matter how much money you have you can't control the weather, stop wars, stop famine and make your relatives less serpentine.

You are not God and until you realize that you will continue to control things you can't. Your problems will still be there. You will still feel insecure with thousands of dollars in your account. You will still feel worthless with money and no matter how many people know you, you will still feel lonely.

Find a way to build yourself up if you want to be successful. Relying on money to solve your problems won't get you far.

# When you are successful you don't need to learn

Success is based on the principles of continuous learning and developing. Successful people have coaches who help them work on their problems. They read tirelessly and are constantly are on the lookout of developing themselves.

Educating yourself never stops. I thought that after college I didn't need to pick up another book to save my life. If you want to better yourself you must be willing to learn and learn and never stop. That's the only way you can develop yourself.

## The Last Battle

I have learned a lot along the way, it's been a battle of figuring who I am to discovering the path I should take. I have had to battle with doubts, insecurities and face my fears. At times, I have fallen and had to find out how to pick myself back up.

If I told you it was easy, it would be a lie. For so long, I had no clue who I was and that terrified me. Not knowing my potential stopped me from discovering who I could become. It took my friend dying for me to begin figuring out who I am.

I don't know your story, your battles or who you are. What I do know is we all have battles that we are facing. At times, those battles can pull us apart and make us doubt who we are and what we are meant to achieve in life.

No one can tell you who you should be and where you must go. I can't tell you what your story is and how it would be written. The main purpose of this book is just a guideline to figure out who you are and what you can achieve. I've had to ask myself time and time again if my life was worth anything. My conclusion to that is yes. The worst part of your life can also be the best because it is there that you will be tested and figure out who you are.

When you get there. You ask yourself questions that appear daunting but are not. You are worthy of success and greatness. We have one life and that may seem like we have time, but we don't. Live your life with boldness and believe you can make a difference. Believe that God put you on earth for a reason. Know that you are important and you have a story worth telling.

Write a book, join a cause, ask yourself questions that are daunting and live a life full of no regret. This book is for all those who feel worthless, the rejects, those who have given up, those who have lost faith in themselves and people. I wrote this book because at one point in time I felt worthless. I felt rejected and I felt as though ending my life would make the worth better.

You are worth more than you think.

# About the Author

Vanessa Gowora is a lifestyle entrepreneur, business coach, and motivational speaker. She helps millennials figure out their why, build businesses around their passions and live life to their full potential. This is the first book in her Success Mastery Series.

Vanessagowora.com

# Acknowledgments

This book wouldn't have been possible without the support of all my family and friends who guided me and gave me advice when writing the book.

To my family who didn't truly understand why I was writing this book but supported me regardless of that fact. Thank you, big sister(Nyasha Gowora), for your advice when I was writing this book. I wouldn't have finished without your input. Thank you, mom and dad, who kept uplifting my spirits as I was writing this. Thank you to my brother who without a doubt gave me a nudge when I needed it. To all my cousins thank you for your support(Eve Mungoni, Kevin King and the poet of the family, Shawn Mahasi.)

This book wouldn't have come to fruition if it wasn't for all my friends who stood by through everything. You all inspired me to write this book and even if I didn't mention you in the book, know that all of this wouldn't have been possible without you all. Takudzwa Chipanga, Nazeema Kassim, Ruvarashe Beta, CJ Peirson, Natasha Saungweme, Nelia Chibanda, Makenna Mahlangu, Precious Jakaza, Kudzai Lamboz, Tafadzwa Mushaninga, Shingai Nyemba, Bianca Kutepa, Chioiso Makuwaza, and Michelle Kuchocha Muchehiwa.

# One Last Time

It would be really awesome if you can leave me an honest review on Amazon letting me know what you thought about the book.

If you want to find out how you can make your life better, follow your dreams and become a better version of yourself click the link below.

Thanks

Vanessa Gowora